PROPERTY PROSPERITY

7 Steps to Investing Like an Expert

Published in 2013 in Australia by Property Mavens Pty Ltd
Revised in March 2016

miriam@propertymavens.com.au
www.propertymavens.com.au

Book Production: OpenBook Creative
Cover Design: Peter Reardon
Cover Image: Beth Jennings Photography
Editor: Jacqui Pretty

National Library of Australia Cataloguing-in-Publication entry (pbk)
Author: Sandkuhler, Miriam, author.
Title: Property prosperity : 7 steps to investing like an expert / Miriam Sandkuhler.
ISBN: 9780992378240 (paperback)
           9780992378257 (ebook : epub)
           9780992378264 (ebook : kindle)
Subjects: Real estate investment--Australia.
Real estate business--Australia.
Dewey Number: 332.63240994

PROPERTY PROSPERITY

7 Steps to Investing Like an Expert

Miriam Sandkuhler

Praise for **Property Prosperity
– 7 Steps to Investing like an Expert**

"I read with a highlighter pen and mark passages that strongly resonate.

I've marked more passages in Property Prosperity than any other real estate book I've read in the past five years. I find myself agreeing with a lot of the things you write.

It's a logical, knowledgeable and ethical approach to property investment from someone who clearly knows the business. I value sensible, ethical, well-written advice and this book is full of it."

—Terry Ryder, M.D. Hotspotting, Journalist

'Like a pair of goggles that change the way you look at real estate! Most people approach property like a customer. They do what the bank wants, they buy the product the developer wants to sell, they get convinced by an experienced real estate sales person. This book flips things around and gives you the eyes and ears of a professional property investor. You step out of the retail customer mindset and into the mindset of a person who will make money from their property decisions.'

—Daniel Priestly, Entreprenuer, International Bestselling Author

Miriam Sandkuhler is an extraordinary real estate professional.

She is passionate about helping people to make smart investment decisions and this passion comes out in "Property Prosperity".

Her advice is straight forward, filled with integrity and common sense, and clearly, Miriam has the readers best interest at heart every step of the way. A hugely valuable book for anyone who wants to be successful and prosperous in the complex world of property investing.

—Andrew Griffiths, International Bestselling Author

'As an experienced, though by no means expert, property investor in Australia, I wasn't sure whether *Property Prosperity* would be pitched at my level or too high or too simplistic. I was delighted when it arrived to see that the volume of information it contained managed to express some of the 'basics', as well as specific processes and charts that will help me with my next purchase and onwards towards prosperity.

Miriam is not just knowledgeable in the area of property investment - she brings a realism that many other "Get Rich with Property, No Money Down" style books seem to gloss over. As a guide for those who want to build wealth with property and keep it, I can (and have) recommend *Property Prosperity*'.

—Jacob Aldridge, Business Coach

'When everyone else was congratulating me on buying my first property, as a new investor I found myself questioning my decision, very stressed and looking for a way out.

After reading *Property Prosperity*, not only did I realise that I'd made the wrong decision for my level of personal risk, but I was also using the wrong strategy for my income level! No wonder I was stressed!

Now I know I'm armed with the knowledge to make a much better decision next time around.

Property Prosperity is a must-have for anyone considering investing in property.'

—Jacqueline Pretty, Writer/First time Investor

'*Property Prosperity* is simple, straightforward, concise and clear, step by step advice that when applied guarantees a sound investment for any start up investor, no matter age or education.

Not only is there great value in this book but many great values that you will come to trust as your compass when steering the course of your property prosperity future. If you are considering a property purchase of any kind you will learn, what you don't know, what you need to know, and the order in which to chart your individual course. When it comes to investing for your future one size fits all advice does not fit all.

Gaining the knowledge to be strategy specific and responsible in this financial arena is the hallmark of this considered rewarding and insightful new book.'

—Laura Hamilton, Artistic Producer and Live Performance Coach

'It's always refreshing to hear the truth!

Having been a Partner in a full service firm for many years I've seen the successes and failures of property investing. Miriam highlights the difference between sales spruiking and good old fashion independent advice.

After reading *Property Prosperity* you'll make your next purchase with your eyes wide open.'

—Michelle Griffiths, Chartered Accountant

'As a chartered accountant with numerous investment properties, the greatest impact on me is that I can recognise some of the mistakes I have made from reading the commentary in the book *Property Prosperity*.

The seven steps reiterate to me that property investment is not about being lucky by getting in at the right time, but a combination of all these points, and the fact that it makes sense to get advice in the areas which you don't fully understand or just do not have the time to dedicate to the process.

I believe all property investors, even the ones with experience, should review the seven steps prior to making decisions, just to remind themselves of the process.'

—Greg Rozenberg, Taxation and Business Advisor

'An unbiased and honest opinion on how to buy investment property the right way, eliminate costly mistakes other people make, and not have the wool pulled over your eyes by people you thought were trustworthy. A must read for anyone wanting to get onto the property ladder, and unsure where to start. I will be happy to refer my clients and friends to this book, and Miriam's service.

I own a number of investment properties in Australia and overseas and started investing 12 years ago.

Any first time investor, first home buyer, or investor with a small portfolio with a desire to grow their portfolio will benefit from reading this book.'

—Monica van Riet, Property Investor and Mortgage Broker

'I thought my knowledge of property investing was reasonable, although I've not been quite confident enough to put it into practice. Just as well I didn't!

After reading *Property Prosperity* I realised some crucial steps would have been missed (microeconomic indicators and the importance of a building and pest inspector for a start) and my hard earned dollars would have been at risk.

Miriam has written a refreshingly frank and honest property investor bible in *Property Prosperity*, including a great toolkit to inform you of the risks and rewards when investing in this market. She is a property specialist passionate about the 'civilities' of fair play and she walks the talk

Thanks to Miriam, I am now armed with the essentials to get my portfolio started.'

—Mandy Knight, Soon to be Property Investor.

Acknowledgements

For

For my gorgeous nieces Isabella and Holly Sandkuhler. I hope that I can support and encourage you both to become financially independent young women, so that you can live with gratitude and enjoy the freedom that financial independence brings, while also encouraging and supporting others to do the same.

Thank You

I would like to thank the following people for their support during the course of my writing this book. Some have contributed to and/or reviewed content, others have provided the foundation for me to have developed my area of expertise and some have provided guidance along the way, especially when I hit the proverbial (writing) wall.

Damian Collins – for being an inspiration and highly respected role model in the real estate industry, especially in the specialist area of Buyer Advocacy. The industry needs more leaders and innovators like you! I consider myself privileged to have been on your team, where I was able to hone my craft under your highly successful business model.

Emma Everett - for being an inspiration and role model in the profession of Buyer Advocacy and a valued and highly respected friend. The real estate industry needs more women and role models like you!

Andrew Griffiths – you are a legendary author and writing coach. You were right – everyone has a book in them waiting to be written!

Daniel Priestly and Glen Carlson – for creating the KPI program for entrepreneurs like myself and providing us with the tools and system to follow. Like everything in life, you get out of it what you put into it!

Ben Harvey – for creating the Authentic Education programs and reminding me that in being true to myself by being transparent, honest and authentic, I will attract clients who will respect and seek to work with those qualities in me and what my business Property Mavens represents. And yes – I am allowed!

Rosemary Johnston, Mandi Morison, Greg Rozenberg, Obu Ramaraj, Rob Rogers, Katrina Weidemann , Colin Robertson and Michelle Griffiths – thank you all for your 'expert' input and review.

Jacqui Pretty – for your fabulous editing. I may have lost a few thousand words in the edit, but I attained a much better book for it!

Table of Contents

Foreword xvii

Introduction 1

Step 1: Fix Your Money Mindset 29

Step 2: Understand Your Risk 39

Step 3: Develop a Strategy 65

Step 4: Engage Your Team of Experts 87

Step 5: Research, Select and Assess 131

Step 6: Negotiate the Offer 167

Step 7: Review Your Portfolio 191

Conclusion 203

Appendix 1: Methods of Property Sales 211

Appendix 2: Useful Resources 217

Appendix 3: Common Property Investment
        and Development Risks 229

Appendix 4: Tables 239

Glossary of Terms 242

Index 252

Foreword

In December 2015 the Australian residential property market was valued at $5.7 trillion.[1] At the same time, the stock market was valued at only $1.81 trillion. This makes the property market the most valuable market in Australia, forming the foundation of our personal wealth, and our banking sector's security against its funds.

However, unlike the financial planning, insurance and mortgage broking sectors, property as an investment asset is **unregulated**. This means that there is no national regulatory body (like the Australian Securities and Investments Commission) that requires 'factual' claims be based in evidence. Instead we have marketing 'puffery' rather than genuine guidance, where a real estate agent seeks to enhance the appeal of a property to promote its sale. This is deemed perfectly reasonable for home sales that are based on evoking the emotional appeal of the buyer.

---

1 RP Data Capital Market Report 2012, 'Written by Miriam Sandkuhler and Rosemary Johnston, October 2012 Statistics updated as at December 2015

Property for investment, on the other hand, should be considered very differently. Property investment is a business, and it needs to be treated as such. Property for investment needs to be considered on the basis of the potential performance against market averages, not a buyer's emotional whims. To support this we need:

- Standardised formats for claims of historical performance,
- Benchmarks so we can rate if it was above or below average performance, and
- Realistic foundations for future claims (rather than the 'BS' claimed by some developers for local projects).

We are currently lacking in these business standards and enough professionals who understand the nature of this information and can present it in layman's terms. To support transparent decision making, we also need modelling tools that can represent the real estimates for projected cash flow when buying, holding and selling the property. This gives you a virtual test on whether it meets your actual and budgeted 'pocket'.

What investors need is suitably qualified and trusted professionals to give property investment advice that supports their wealth creation. To achieve this, investors need a custodian of their personalised property investment strategy, with sustainable investment entry, holding and exit outcomes. They need risk mitigation support so they can hold a property over their lifetime and realise the benefits as retirement income. This will support their successful wealth creation and enable them to become a strong cohort of independently funded retirees, removing that social responsibility from the Government coffers.

However, most investors don't have access to such professionals. In all states and territories, when a real estate agent acts for the Vendor/Seller, they are prohibited by law from acting for the Purchaser/Buyer in the same transaction. Currently most so called property investment advice services are offered by Vendor/Selling agents without disclosure of their vested interests – i.e. they aren't telling investors they are working for the Vendor by making a commission.

What's wrong with that you may ask? Well, in all states it's against the law not to disclose the vested interest. I question why would they go to all that effort to not be transparent to the buyer, if what they were selling was so fantastic?

What is vital that you take away from this is that you need to know the necessary questions to ask, to understand what you are being presented, and to understand who the presenter represents in the transaction. From here, you will be better prepared to make informed decisions.

Introduction

Free Advice is Never Free

Flip open any property magazine and they all scream with attention-grabbing headlines such as:

- How to invest on a low income
- How to make millions fast
- Single mother becomes property millionaire in 18 months
- Build a multi-million dollar property portfolio in your spare time
- Invest from only $50 per week
- Top 200 suburbs under $300,000
- How to invest with little or no deposit
- Secret strategies of the wealthy
- Quit your day job! How to make $200,000 per annum on the side
- You too can become property wealthy with no effort, no deposit, no money and no knowledge (actually I made that one up for fun…)

Property investing has become so trivialised and it seems so easy, that apparently almost anyone with no experience, no deposit and no income can become a property millionaire – overnight!

What these magazines don't tell you (because their advertisers would be very unhappy about it) is how frequently the property game turns bad for many investors, because they don't know what they don't know.

The people selling property to them aren't required to (and aren't going to) volunteer answers to questions investors don't know to ask, because it may kill their deal and, if they are commission sales agents, they need to eat!

The reality is anyone can sign a contract and 'buy' a property – easy! What's a bit more complicated are the many steps along the way and the due diligence required to ensure you are buying the right type of property for the right reasons and for the right price, which matches your risk profile, goals and personal circumstances.

Free advice is never free …
What does this actually mean?

Exactly that. The commercial reality is that EVERYONE is selling something, myself included. I 'sell' services – qualified and Accredited Property Investment Advice, Buyer Advocacy and Property Portfolio Review services on a fee for service basis. I therefore legally act for my clients and work in their best interests. My advice is transparent, unbiased and impartial. I also have professional indemnity insurance that covers me for the formal provision of such 'property investment advice' by an Accredited Property Investment Advisor.

As the property sector is not regulated by a national governing body such as ASIC (Australian Security and Investments Commission), alarmingly there is no requirement for people involved in the property sector to have a minimum qualification to provide 'property advice'. Therefore there is an abundance of property spruikers, selling agents, wholesale marketers, 'experts', project marketers, seminar presenters, investor clubs, Meetup groups, developers, builders, 'mum and dad' experts, property institutes, 'one-stop-shop' specialists and some financial planners, accountants and mortgage brokers who are all selling property based on the free education, strategy and advice they provide. This education often takes the buyer down the path of buying whatever property or strategy the 'expert' has to sell (the exception is those who offer genuine Buyer Advocacy services – refer to Step 4 Engage Your Team of Experts).

The image below highlights the two sides of the property investing model that currently operates in Australia. There is the 'property model' on the right side, where the vendor is represented by the selling agent who legally represents the vendor's interests. All advice provided to the buyer is free (because a real estate agent can't derive income from both parties to a real estate transaction), but it is usually biased too. This side of the property investing model is highly predominant in the marketplace and operates throughout Australia.

The 'advice model' is represented on the left, where the buyer is represented by a Buyer Agent or Accredited Property Investment Advisor who legally represents their interests. In both cases, all advice is fee for service. Because fees are transparent and your buyer agent isn't getting a commission or incentive to sell you a property, you can rest assured that your best interests at heart. This side of the property investing model has a much, much smaller representation throughout Australia.

Advice Model (Buying)	Buyer Agent	Selling Agent	Property Model (Selling)
• INDEPENDENT and UNBIASED advice			• PREJUDICED and BIASED advice
• Fee for service			• Often 'free' advice (for which you will usually pay down the track)
• Offers tailored advice or service	Accredited Property Investment Advisor	Project Marketer	• Property driven advice, while it may be tailored it is always based on only the property they have to sell
• Strategy driven advice, not property driven advice			

Figure 1 The two sides of the Property Investing Model

A) The **unbiased** Advice Model usually always starts with a **needs analysis** to create a **strategy** to help you, the investor, fulfil your needs or goals.

Then you are presented with the **solution**, or the property type used to carry out your strategy.

The next step is that the **marketplace is researched to source** property for you that matches your tailored strategy, and you pay them a fee for the services provided.

B) On the **biased** Property Model side, agents may or may not start with a **needs analysis** to create a **strategy**. They will then present you with the **solution** (the property type) which they often have to **sell** you from **a selection of new or off the plan developer stock**. Because they are creating a strategy with a solution already in mind (the property sale from which they'll receive a commission), this information and these recommendations can never truly be impartial

No matter how nice, kind, helpful they are, no matter how many 'independent' research reports they provide (check who paid for the research – typically it was the developer, therefore they aren't actually 'independent'), they are **never unbiased or impartial**. Even if they charge you a fee for the strategy they provide, if it results in the recommendation of buying the property they are selling, it is still biased 'property based' advice.

What's wrong with the Property Model? Well nothing, providing it is **transparent** and that you are fully aware that their main interest lies in whether or not you are a qualified buyer. If you have adequate savings or equity (for a deposit) and the cash or ability to qualify for finance to afford your investment, that's all they're looking for.

They are unlikely to take into account or provide you with hold or exit strategies, and most likely also won't consider your risk profile, individual age(s), marital status, number of dependents (children or otherwise), timeframes and overall debt levels. In other words, any 'education', 'strategy' or 'advice' you receive is often not tailored to your specific circumstances. Its purpose is to sell you the stock that they have to sell. They are presenting you with a one size fits all solution.

This isn't to say they don't genuinely want to help people create wealth, but it does mean they can only do it based on the property/development/stock they have listed for sale. This is true of everyone selling property, whether they are a local real estate agent, developer, builder, project marketer or your friendly accountant, financial planner, lawyer or mortgage broker who 'refers' you to a property partner/in-house associate, while earning commissions (marketing fees) or referral fees for each client that is 'sold' a property along the way.

Please note, these commissions (marketing fees) and referral fees are all **built into and therefore inflate** the property price, which means you are often overpaying for the property in the first instance and therefore the advice isn't actually free after all. The cost is simply hidden and it can mean in a flat or declining market that when it comes time to settle, the value of the property could have decreased, so you need to find a bigger deposit or you may not be able to settle at all.

Marketing Terminology and Puffery

Unlike the financial planning, insurance and mortgage broking sectors, property as an investment asset is **unregulated** – i.e. there is no single national regulatory body (such as ASIC) that requires that factual claims be based in evidence. Claims can't however be misleading or deceptive, otherwise the Department of Consumer Affairs or Fair Trading in your local state can investigate on behalf of a claimant.

Rather we have 'puffery', where a real estate agent seeks to enhance the appeal of a property to promote its sale. This is deemed perfectly reasonable for owner-occupied home sales, which are based on evoking the emotional appeal of the buyer. Property for investment, however, should be considered very differently. It needs to be considered on the basis of the potential performance against market averages, NOT a property's emotional appeal.

In short, be wary of the following types of statements, which are designed to play to buyers' emotions:

- Pay 'Wholesale' not 'Retail' prices for the property (there is actually no such thing as 'Wholesale' prices)

- Access property wholesale before the general public

- Invest in some of Australia's fastest growing 'hot spots' with strong potential return on investment (ROI) and high capital growth

- Invest in properties designed by award-winning architects at significantly discounted prices

- Secret strategies you need to know about to make your fortune in property (and keep it!)

- Fastest growing region in the state

- Land banking – the latest 'secret' way to become rich

- Investor membership fees will be reimbursed upon the purchase of a property

- Get paid to invest in property

- Align yourself with our leading property sourcing team so you benefit from access to the most lucrative 'silent sales' on the market, where you can access pre-release deals that are often not available to the general public

- Let us mentor (or coach) you to property success

- We find out what you are looking for in an investment property. Then we go and 'find' that property for you. When we have it, we present it to you along with all the supporting documents and information you need before you buy it. Our goal is to make property investing simple.

Emotive language can also be used to lend a false sense of security, with words and phrases such as safely, carefully, delivering the best possible result, working for you, our buyer managers, our investor buyer's agency etc.

'Free' Services and How they are Really Paid

There are numerous clever and innovative ways of selling property in the marketplace today, including memberships, referrers, research houses, telemarketing/in-home visits, clubs, mentoring/coaching and property 'experts'. Urgency and exclusivity are often used in many of these sales methods to put pressure on buyers to make fast decisions, without allowing them time to seek independent advice on the basis that they will miss out.

The reality is, however, that there is always another property around the corner and, in flatter markets, the so called urgency isn't warranted UNLESS they can genuinely show you what makes their property unique, boutique or highly desirable and in high demand.

Often these methods educate their clients to buy their product, but they may not provide holistic advice.

Memberships

One method is offering memberships to investors' groups, project marketing firms or clubs for exclusive access to special deals that have been sourced by specialist acquisition teams who negotiate amazing deals on behalf of their members/buyers.

Sound familiar? DON'T BE FOOLED. In its simplest form this is sales and marketing 'smoke and mirrors' to hide the fact that they are real estate sales agents/project marketers/property spruikers/wholesalers of property. While they might sound like they are working for you and your interests, they are actually being paid by a vendor/seller/developer and are seeking the highest sale price possible. They are acting in the Vendor's best interests at all times, not yours!

Again, there is protection for consumers against deceptive and misleading conduct under the trade practices or fair trading legislation. If you feel this has transpired, please report these memberships to Consumer Affairs/Fair Trading for investigation.

Case Study – *Susan*

Susan attended an all-day property road show/seminar recently, at which three property 'experts' were presenting. One specialised in teaching investors to renovate and was transparent and upfront about the service and fees offered. One specialised in mentoring services and made it clear their company didn't buy or sell property. The last 'expert' pulled out all the smoke and mirrors and did the exact opposite. The presentation was formulaic and designed to wow, evoke emotion, create urgency and take people down the path of visualising a better life. The way into this better life? Jumping on board with their 'secret' strategy (land banking).

It just so happened that the language used by the presenter in the script didn't match the data presented on the slides (to support the reasons why people should invest in this amazing strategy). For example, they were selling 'land' but the presenter only referred to 'property' when citing examples of massive growth historically and referred to 'land' when it suited the sales presentation. It also just so happened that the historical growth and supporting articles shown were seven years out of date and there was no reference to the source of some statistics, so no one had the ability to do any independent verification.

There was a 'limited' offer to join as a member by paying $3995, which would be used as a deposit when the 'member' proceeded to buy a property. There were limited appointments available with property coaches, who would provide a free consultation to explain the amazing concept and tailor a strategy to attendees' needs.

At the end of the presentation, Susan spoke directly to the presenter and asked if he was a buyer agent and he said no (even though his marketing materials referred to him as a buyer agent)! She asked how his company got paid and he said they received a 'marketing fee'. She qualified if it was a sales commission and he said he wasn't a selling agent (but he used to be a buyer agent)! She asked again if his company was a licensed real estate agency that received a sales commission when property was sold and after several minutes of back and forth he finally admitted that was the case – they were a commission-based real estate agency that sold land. What an effort to get a straight answer!

This guy was the perfect example of why real estate agents get a bad reputation due to this lack of transparency!

As at January 2016, the property 'expert' referred to has been identified as working for a high profile disreputable property spruiker.

ASIC is investigating claims of this latest property scam, with a Senate inquiry probing into the marketing and advice offered re the land banking 'schemes'.

A class action is also being considered (against the promoters), by disgruntled investors.

Referrers

Referrers are professionals who refer their clients internally or externally to real estate marketers or promoters, and receive commissions each time one of their clients buys a property through the referred group. These professionals may include (but aren't limited to) accountants, financial planners, mortgage brokers and lawyers.

They work either directly with developers or via property 'wholesale', 'aggregator' or 'project marketing' groups who act as the facilitators of the sales process. The wholesaler/project marketer 'lists' for sale properties from developers, distributing them to the hundreds or thousands of a professional's unsuspecting clients, while giving the referrer a massive commission (1 – 8% of the sale price) and taking a cut for themselves in the process.

These so called 'exclusive' property opportunities are often 'off market' and not released to the 'retail' market until the 'wholesale' market has been fully exploited: i.e. they attempt to get rid of as much of their stock as possible in the first instance via wholesale distribution channels, so that they can go the 'retail' market with what's left, bragging that X% is already sold. This leaves the general public to soak up the balance of the remaining stock and often unaware that the best properties have already been picked over and sold.

Referrers really need to understand the needs of their clients, who they are referring their clients to and how they're making themselves vulnerable to potential litigation in the process. It is concerning that many referrers are effectively selling their clients down the river without necessarily knowing it, based on them often being sold property that ultimately doesn't stack up as a good investment and leaving their clients in a worse financial position than when they were first 'introduced' to the wholesaler/aggregator/project marketer/ research house/club/Meetup group, etc. I have often seen clients in this predicament, lumbered with poor performing property, a loss of equity, the inability to exit the situation easily or quickly, and uncertainty and stress about how to move forward.

Note – the term 'wholesale' doesn't refer to a discount on property, it refers to a method of distribution. No developer will ever 'discount' property to sell it faster. That's where enticements come in!

See Appendix 1 – Methods of Property Sale to learn more about how Referral strategies work.

Research Houses

Research Houses are often licensed real estate agencies marketing themselves as 'research' houses, or having specialist property research or acquisitions teams within their firm, who source or assess developments presented to them. They determine whether these developments meet particular criteria required for them to be willing to sell them to their clients or referral partners/business partners. On the plus side, some of these firms are being more selective with the property they are selling than the average project marketer, but they are still selling from the limited selection that they have, and not from the total marketplace.

You are likely to be invited by your accountant or financial planner to attend a research house's Property Market update, where you can learn how to accelerate wealth personally or via a Self-Managed Superfund (SMSF) by investing in property. You can also discover the key drivers of capital growth, understand property cycles and the importance of investing at the right time (which will be immediately because they have stock to sell immediately) and discover growth markets and buying opportunities (the stock they have on hand).

Example – It goes something like this
We provide customised investment strategies based on your personal goals and situation. By providing professional advice about your investment needs and **exclusive access to properties** that have been sourced and negotiated by our specialist *investor buyer agency**, we help you to achieve your property goals without stress or fuss.

---

* It is possible that use of terminology such as 'investor buyer agency' when they are in fact acting as for a seller or vendor could be deemed deceptive and misleading conduct by Consumer Affairs/Fair Trading, so ask questions to clarify how they are being paid. If you feel they are blatantly misleading the public, you can report them to your local office of Fair Trading/Consumer Affairs or the ACCC (Australian Competition and Consumer Commission).

Telemarketing/In-home visits

You have probably found yourself on the receiving end of a telemarketing call at some point. It is common for project marketing firms to use this practice to invite potential investors to seminars or even book in-home consultations.

Once you have attended the seminar and have been further qualified, a follow up 'strategy' session is booked at the office or in your home and consultants come out to see you and take you down the path of a usually high pressure and fast process to get you to buy property through them.

Clubs

The purpose of many of these groups is to provide education, networking support and often the sourcing and provision of property for purchase. Joining a club is showing an indication that you are self-directed in your desire to buy property. However, it doesn't mean these services are holistic or impartial, because the group's purpose is to sell property to members, not just to educate.

Mentoring/Coaching

Mentors and coaches provide direction and guidance during the process of achieving your goals. Be careful if they are 'mentoring' or 'coaching' you to buy property that they happen to have listed/available for sale

If they are guiding you to go into the marketplace to search for, research and buy your own property, that's different – they truly are mentoring and they may charge you a fee for the service. Note these fees can be very high and with little time allocated for coaching. I have heard of $10,000 fees with only 1 hour of one on one coaching per month. However, if they are guiding you to invest in a specific 'opportunity' (or from a select group of opportunities), then they likely have a vested interest in you buying one of those, which means their advice isn't impartial and it would be best to seek a second (or third!) opinion.

Mentoring and coaching services in property investment sometimes also go by the name of Investment 'institutes', which offer education to investors, which often leads down the path of being sold property.

'Experts'

There are a number of 'experts' in the marketplace who often cite their own personal wealth and the size of their portfolio of property as the example of their 'expertise'. They may provide regular commentary in the marketplace, or they may be highly knowledgeable about property generally across many aspects. The main thing to be aware of is that many 'experts' also develop and/or sell property or gain financially from its sale, so it wouldn't surprise me if, in fact, much of their wealth/property success stemmed from the profits and commissions they have made and continue to make selling real estate, rather than solely from their personal 'investing success story'.

The main point here is to be aware of what they are an 'expert' in and how they derive their income. Is it by providing holistic and impartial advice, or is there property for sale attached to their 'expert' advice? And when they provide buying tips to investors, how much information are they most likely holding back on?

OTHER FORMS OF INFLUENCE
Magazines

These are often a source of primary education and help to set the expectation of property buyers (whether realistic or not) and act as the vehicle to distribute advertising materials and offers on behalf of their clients via advertorials, email campaigns or magazine advertisements. They fuel the appetite and are selling a pipedream to investors.

They do provide independent information across a number of relevant property-related sectors, such as accounting, broking and quantity surveying, and they do include articles written by fee for service buyer agents and professionals as well as selling agents, but they also provide the platform to market property for sale to the thousands of subscribers on their databases.

Real Estate/Selling Agents

Just as a solicitor can act for the defendant or the plaintiff/ prosecution in a legal matter, a Licensed Estate Agent can act/work for the buyer or the vendor (seller) in a property transaction, but never both at the same time.

Your local neighbourhood selling agent is the source of most of the established property for sale in the marketplace. They are paid by and represent their vendor in the property transaction, which is a totally transparent process.

However, they are trained not to sell 'property' per se, but to sell 'hopes and dreams'.

Industry events and workshops exist to help agents sharpen skills to generate stronger results; more sales and higher auction clearance rates.

When seeking advice from a real estate sales agent and using the solicitor analogy above, remember, asking a selling agent for advice when buying property is like going to court to fight criminal charges, but without engaging a solicitor to defend you, and then also asking the prosecutor for advice!

Enticements

As potential homebuyers and investors are swamped for choice, property developers and builders are looking for new ways to encourage buyers to purchase property. In quieter markets, with substandard property, an oversupply of local stock, or as part of the style of property (e.g. resort-style short -stay property), these 'extras' or bonuses can add up to tens of thousands worth of extra value. Note that the extra value is usually built into the purchase price so you, as a buyer, are actually paying for it in one form or another.

These enticements often include things such as frequent flyer points, holidays, furniture packages, cars, marina berths, rental guarantees, stamp-duty offsets, mortgage offsets, dinners, spa treatments, golf or gym memberships, personal usage days per annum (for resort-style short-stay property), first home owner grant boosts and the list goes on!

Sales techniques are used frequently to distract investors from a property's poor investment fundamentals. Tax benefits such as depreciation and negative gearing, and now even Self-Managed Superfunds structures are used to encourage investors to purchase property that often isn't investment grade.

To physically get you to a property site to experience the lifestyle, these enticements could include free boat rides, flights, and a weekend away stay. Other project marketers offer you retail gift cards, concert tickets, and discounted flights to attend a 90-minute seminar so they can take you through their sales presentation. Rest assured these are highly crafted high pressure environments designed to create urgency and take investors down a path that they struggle to escape from because techniques like neuro linguistic programming (NLP) and highly developed sales scripts are designed to get you to sign on the dotted line. Anything designed to get you hyped up and excited to buy is something to be wary of and you should proceed with caution. Other investment products such as shares and managed investments are never allowed to be sold using these methods, due to those sectors being regulated by ASIC, so buyer beware.

Other property promoters will align themselves with other professionals to become one-stop-shops, such as having financial planners, accountants, property managers and lenders in-house so that it's easy and seamless for you. However, the purpose is also so that they can manage and control you through the whole sales process, ensuring you won't get independent advice elsewhere, cool off and possibly pull out of the deal.

Be Aware

Be aware, if they are charging you a fee that covers everything from 'finding' you a property to handling the finance and conveyancing AND they are presenting developer stock to you from a pool of property they have exclusive access to (but they aren't being paid by the developer because you are paying them), then my attitude is that they are behaving like a project marketer, but call themselves a 'buyer advocate'. This is because technically, you are paying for the 'package of services' they have created and, effectively, the privilege of being associated with them.

How Do You Know If It's The 'Real Deal' or 'Too Good to Be True'?

As you can see, there is a lack of transparency in the Australian property marketplace, with a range of 'smoke and mirror' sales and marketing methods that are used to entice buyers into investing in properties that aren't always investment grade or high performing.

With so much puffery and so many innovative ways of selling property, how do you, as a buyer, know whether or not you're not only getting a good deal, but an investment-grade property that will grow in value over time and provide you and your family with financial security for the future? This is the goal of this book.

I wrote *Property Prosperity - 7 Steps to Investing Like an Expert* as a result of seeing many clients who had made poor property investment choices, often because they were sold a property by a real estate sales agent under the guise of it being a 'good investment'. The buyer, however, either did no independent research or had no real understanding of the risks. They didn't understand their own risk profile or that of the property, its real opportunity to grow in value over time, if it would secure a good tenant, if it would continually generate a strong income and if they could easily dispose of the property when they wanted to cash out.

Throughout the following chapters, it is my hope that you gain a better understanding of what makes a successful and prosperous property investor. By understanding the importance of approaching investing from the perspective of it being a business and a sustainable investment i.e. one that you can enter into, hold onto long term and exit out of easily, while having it achieve your goals, I hope you will enjoy property prosperity in your lifetime.

Some of what you read may be confronting or challenge your thinking, but the intent is for you to become informed and empowered, so that you can make better investment decisions in the future. It's not about scaring you into taking no action, but about you making decisions based on knowing your personal risk profile, property risk profile and investing accordingly using independently sourced research and information.

If even just one investor makes better informed choices when spending hundreds of thousands of their hard-earned cash as result or reading my book, then I have achieved my objective and will be thrilled!

Wishing you a prosperous property investing outcome,

Miriam

KEY POINTS

- Remember free advice is never free - you may pay at some point down the track and how you pay can often be the concern (refer to the Capital Growth chart in Step 2). You may 'pay' by losing out on thousands of dollars of capital growth over time or by not being able to easily resell the property down the track.

- Ask questions to determine if the marketing hype is really a way of covering a lack of impartiality.

- Always do your own due diligence and research as back up to the so called 'independent' research provided.

- All of the parties referred to in the Property model have a vested interest in your entering the property market, however they often don't have a vested interest (with the exception of mortgage brokers) in you holding or exiting the property, so buyer beware.

STEP 1

Fix Your Money Mindset

"If you can't manage your emotions, don't expect to be able to manage your money."
– **Warren Buffet**

You may be wondering – what does money mindset have to do with property investment?

While it's important to have goals, think positively, visualise your outcome and surround yourself with likeminded people who inspire you to create a better life or lifestyle; it is also important to recognise that many of us have limiting belief systems. These limiting beliefs undermine our efforts to create that better life we desire, for both ourselves and our loved ones.

Have you ever wondered why some people just can't seem to get ahead financially? No matter what they try, it never seems to work out. Conversely, why do other people, who aren't as smart or don't work as hard, seem to have all the luck? Or are you one of those people who had it all and then lost it for reasons beyond your control, and you can't seem to get back on your feet?

While I have no formal qualifications in the area of psychology, I have participated in a variety of different personal development courses and read a multitude of related books and, based on these studies, I've realised the fundamental role that a person's money mindset plays in their property investment endeavours.

As such, I wanted to share one simple but powerful technique with you before progressing to the nuts and bolts of this book – teaching you how to strategically build a prosperous property portfolio that is sustainable, and tailored to your unique circumstances.

The following content is courtesy of Benjamin J Harvey from Authentic Education.

> 'If you don't learn to master money,
> it will master you'

Often we are trapped in our thinking because we don't allow ourselves to see possibilities. The process here is to enable you to refocus your mind. By posing logical questions to the mind and seeking rational solutions, you are able to avoid the emotional centre responses of the mind – thus negating fear altogether.

EXERCISE

What bothers you about money?

1 Find a quiet place to sit – free from distraction – and grab a pen and some paper.

2 On that paper answer the following questions:
   What does money mean to me?
   What are all the things that bother me about money?

There are no rules and no right or wrong answers with this process. Make the list as long as you like as this is a 'brain dumping' exercise, and don't judge what comes up.

Answers to Question 1 could vary from freedom, relief, peace, fun, choice, travel, and philanthropy to love. While 'love' may sound unusual, at its core money is a gift, and when someone gifts you money, or pays you for services provided, it is an expression of gratitude and appreciation, i.e. a form of love.

Answers for question 2 could range from the risk of losing money, friends being envious, investing it poorly, not being able to pay bills and being unable to survive without it, to paying too much tax. Again remember, there are no rules and no right or wrong answers.

3 Once you have completed question 2, review your answers and ask yourself: 'What do I believe to be true that isn't?' Note – this question and process can be applied to your health, relationships, employment, wealth and other limiting beliefs.

For example, if you are fearful of having money but losing friends as a result of it, you can transform this fear by putting steps in place to dissolve it.

4 Draw the following columns and headings on another sheet of paper and go through the list of 'bothers' that you identified at question 2. Decide which top three bothers cause you the most concern and place those in your table, per the examples below:

My Bother	My Action Question	My Answers
The risk of losing it once I have it		
Friends may take advantage of me		
I have to manage it and am not equipped for that		

5 Complete the next column in the table with your action questions. Here you are using logical thoughts to create new thoughts by removing emotions and replacing them with strategic ideas and thinking.

For the purpose of this exercise, you need to take your fear and reverse it into a positive action step, per the examples below, always starting with the line "How many ways can I … or How do I ……"

My Bother	My Action Question	My Answers
The risk of losing it once I have it	How many ways can I continue to receive massive passive income?	
Friends may take advantage of me	How do I continue to make genuine friends while receiving and generating wealth?	
I have to manage it and am not equipped for that	How many ways can I continue to receive even more money to generate financial security for myself and my family?	

6 The final step is to write down all the solutions that will go towards dissolving the bother/fear that you have, per the examples below. As you fix your money mindset, you'll be free to move forward with your property investing from a clean slate.

My Bother	My Action Question	My Answers
The risk of losing it once I have it	How many ways can I continue to receive massive passive income?	Take out the necessary insurances that I need to protect myself and my assets. Learn about different asset types Engage professionals to help me manage it.
Friends may take advantage of me	How do I continue to make genuine friends while receiving and generating wealth?	Join networking groups with likeminded individuals. Set boundaries so that I can't be taken advantage of. Be humble in my new found wealth.
I have to manage it and am not equipped for that	How many ways can I continue to receive even more money to generate financial security for myself and my family?	Engage professionals to help me manage it. Learn about book keeping, budgeting and cash flow management Start a savings plan.

From here, implement your action steps and keep working through any additional bothers that come up, until the fear or bother that you have dissipates altogether.

As you fix your money mindset, you'll be free to move forward with your property investing from a clean slate.

'The key to change ... is to let go of fear.'
– Rosanne Cash

NOTES

KEY POINTS

- Get your money mindset in check and do the exercises.

- Implement the answers to your action questions.

- Monitor what you have implemented to ensure you have eliminated the limiting belief.

- Regularly check for any other 'bothers' that may come up. Sometimes you need to go through all the layers to get to the core of the 'bother' – a bit like peeling an onion!

Now, read on for the nuts and bolts.

STEP

Understand Your Risk

2

Risk is the extent to which you are willing to expose yourself to loss in return for a particular level of gain.

In movies and the media, people are applauded for taking big risks. They scale mountains, topple governments, reveal conspiracies, get the guy (or girl) and live happily ever after.

In property investment, not so much. When establishing or growing a property portfolio, you need to treat your investments as a business and consider risk as if you were a business owner. Otherwise you're simply gambling.

In my roles as an Accredited Property Investment Advisor and a Buyer Agent (refer to Step 4 Engage Your Team of Experts), I frequently come across clients who inform me that they have a low to moderate risk profile, but they want to get into property development. However, they don't understand that property development is a high risk strategy (refer to Step 5 Research, Select and Assess). While the potential returns of developing appeal, the risk often doesn't, so they rightfully end up revising their investment strategy to match their personal risk profile.

It is essential to understand the relevance of risk during the establishment or growth of your property portfolio as a means of managing and/or mitigating it. At a minimum, it will enable you to make more informed and appropriate investment decisions from the outset and at best it will save you from losing tens or hundreds of thousands of your hard earned equity or savings.

Types of Personal Risk

Given the different types of property, and the fact that their varied risk levels aren't suitable for everyone, it is important to assess your personal risk, just as you would when discussing investing in managed funds or shares with a financial planner.

In addition, property is most often an investor's most expensive purchase. It is the one they rely on the most to leverage, and to succeed in creating financial prosperity for themselves and their family. It would be remiss to not understand your risk profile when purchasing property – this ensures you have the best opportunity for your investment to succeed, as well as keeping your stress levels to a minimum.

EXERCISE

1 Personal risk – gauge what type of investor you (and your partner) are.

Use the table, *Investor Type: What Type of Investor Are You?* in appendix 4 and nominate the type of investor you feel you are. This should correlate with your investment attitude results.

2 Assess and understand your risk profile

Assess and understand your risk profile by using the table, *Investment Attitudes*, in appendix 4 to gauge what your (and your partner's) attitude is to investing. Note, it is important to pay attention to each individual question and how you rate it. This is so you think carefully, rather than flicking though answering each question the same way.

Test Results

Now, add up the total score you have out of 60 to see which way you mostly lean. If your score is:

- 0 – 20 then you have a conservative investment attitude,
- 21 – 30 you have a cautious investment attitude,
- 31 – 40 you have a prudent investment attitude,
- 41 – 50 you have an assertive investment attitude, and
- 51 – 60 you have an aggressive investment attitude.

Conservative
- Being conservative you are risk averse
- Preserving income and capital are very important to you
- Consider investing for yield (income) while protecting your capital
- You need to be able to 'sleep at night' so will forgo higher returns for peace of mind

- You should only invest in standard residential property in capital cities or large regional centres where the drivers for growth are strong
- A very low borrowing Loan to Value ratio (LVR) of 50 – 60% can provide positive cash flow

Cautious

- Being cautious you are prepared to accept some risk
- Security of your funds is important to you as it is an income
- Consider investing for yield (income) while protecting your capital but allowing for the opportunity of capital growth
- You should only invest in standard residential property in capital cities or large regional centres where the drivers for growth are strong
- A low borrowing Loan to Value ratio (LVR) of 60 – 70% can provide neutral to positive cash flow

Prudent

- Being prudent/moderate you are willing to take moderate but calculated risks to achieve higher returns
- Consider investing in standard residential property in capital cities or large regional centres where drivers for growth are strong, however, based on additional due diligence, you could invest in areas where the return if higher and more speculative, such as mining towns, or you could consider a different type of property, such as a residentially zoned short stay apartment in a resort or tourist centre

- A medium borrowing Loan to Value ratio (LVR) of 70 – 80% can provide neutral cash flow to negative gearing

Assertive
- You are an assertive investor and are comfortable with moderate to high levels of calculated risk
- You would invest for capital growth and would utilise negative gearing, with the rental return to help fund the investment
- In addition to standard residential property you would consider renovation and add value concepts to increase the capital value of your property investments and may consider diversifying into other property types such as short-stay holiday rentals, retirement villages or commercial properties such as small serviced offices with strong rental demand
- A high borrowing Loan to Value ratio (LVR) of 80 – 90% will result in high negative gearing

Aggressive
- You are an aggressive investor and are comfortable with very high levels of calculated risk
- You would invest for capital growth and would utilise negative gearing, with the rental return to help fund the investment

- In addition to standard residential property and short stay holiday rentals or retirement villages, you could also consider commercial properties such as small serviced offices with strong rental demand and high returns
- You would consider development concepts such as subdivision and building to increase the capital value of your investments and diversify into commercial and industrial property (consider commercial retail with large franchise tenants or warehouses or factories, providing you do your due diligence to mitigate risk)
- A very high borrowing Loan to Value ratio (LVR) of 90 – 105% will result in very high negative gearing. This is, of course, subject to a lender allowing you to borrow at such a high LVR, most likely using cross-collateralisation, which is also high risk and not recommended

---

1 The risk profiles have been modified from a version created by Margaret Lomas

Level of Involvement

If your involvement level is passive then it is imperative that you engage the services of a professional that can provide evidence of their expertise in the area in which you need their assistance, and if it is active, then you need to ensure you do a lot of due diligence yourself when investing to mitigate risk.

Passive – engage professionals to do the work **for you**

Medium – engage professionals to do the work **with you**

Active – do the work yourself and use professionals to **check your work**

Risk Attitude

1   Use the table, *Risk Attitudes*, in appendix 4 to gauge what your (and your partner's) attitudes are to risk mitigation.

Remember, **risk is the extent to which you are willing to expose yourself to loss in return for a level of gain.** If you score at the low end of risk attitude (mostly 5 or below), think carefully before investing, and ensure you have appropriate risk mitigation strategies in place.

Regardless of whether you score at the low end or high end of risk attitude, to safely and strategically build a prosperous property portfolio, it is wise to mitigate risk as much as possible. This includes taking out the required insurances that you need to protect your assets and income in the event of accident, illness or death, as your family may depend upon that income.

How many times have you turned on the news to see a house burnt down and the owner doesn't have insurance? While we can all feel compassion for someone in this situation, by not having insurance they took a substantial risk, and are suffering substantial emotional and financial consequences as a result.

At an absolute minimum, everyone needs to have income protection as a means of ensuring that you can still pay your bills (including those that insure your car and house!), feed yourself and your family and not have to liquidate your assets, including your home if something happens to you.

In the event of an accident, illness or death, many an investor has been forced not only to sell property, but they have also had to deal with the extra blow of a capital gains tax bill at the same time. And, if selling in a flat market, it may mean they couldn't sell as quickly as they would like, they made little to no capital gain or, worse still, they may have made a loss. Nasty!

A word of warning (and some sage relationship advice): When investing, do it according to the person in the relationship with the lowest or most cautious risk profile.

That way you can both sleep at night, sustain your relationship and avoid fighting over the financial stresses that occur in many relationships when each partner has a different investment and risk profile and the more conservative partner is pushed past their comfort level. This applies whether you are investing with a spouse, family member, business partner or friend.

Risk Appetite

According to the Property Investment Association of Australia's (PIAA) Property Investment Advice Course, risk appetite is a person's desire to take action. Someone with a low risk appetite may be satisfied with buying only one investment property, whereas someone with a high risk appetite may want to buy 10 or more.

It's not just the quantity to consider, but the level of due diligence an investor is willing to perform to obtain their desired outcome. Due diligence is the degree of care and research, investigation and risk mitigation you are willing to do to protect your interests when purchasing property.

Conflicts arise when a person with a low risk profile has a high risk appetite. If they are naturally conservative or cautious and fear taking action, it is unlikely they will achieve their objective regardless of their desire. This is where working with an expert buyer advocate can help them achieve their goals.

Conversely, someone with a high risk profile and high risk appetite is likely to race out there and accumulate as much property as possible as quickly as possible, while possibly foregoing due diligence in the process.

Case Study – *Stewart*

Stewart had acquired a half share in four properties with his brother and wanted to keep accumulating while his brother wanted to put the brakes on for a while (different risk appetites).

Stewart decided to go it alone and having bought 50% of four yield-driven properties he felt he was knowledgeable enough to go out on his own and buy a very expensive capital growth property to live in.

We were aware of the auction he was bidding at and later found out that an industry colleague was also bidding for her client at the same auction. Her client had done his due diligence before the auction (building and pest inspections) whereas Stewart hadn't (he was a carpenter so he felt his superficial assessment was sufficient).

Fortunately for Stewart, he missed out on buying the property. Unbeknownst to him, there had been a subfloor fire in the property that caused some structural concerns and required repair work. The other bidder made a calculated decision to proceed within a budget to allow for repairs, whereas Stewart decided to rock up on the day, not certain if he would bid or not. Had he bid and secured the property, he would have inherited a very expensive problem because his high risk profile, high risk appetite, and a little bit too much confidence got in his way. An extra $15,000 - $25,000 worth of unexpected costs could have made all the difference between buying well versus buying poorly and effectively paying too much for the property.

Having bought 50% of four rental income properties, he now wanted to go it alone and buy several more properties under his own steam.

What he didn't consider were the implications of the joint purchases with his brother from a lending perspective. As all of his loans were set up as 'joint and severally liable' (this means the bank considered him responsible for 100% of the debt repayments from a servicing perspective), this severely limited his borrowing capacity for future purchases. Had he engaged an accredited property investment advisor and a mortgage broker who specialised in structuring loans for large property/investment portfolios (more on this in Step 4) and taken both his and his brother's risk appetites into consideration BEFORE buying four properties together, he could have avoided this problem by buying fewer properties with his brother and more in his own name.

In addition, he and his brother had no discussion or agreement as to what would happen with the property when both of their circumstances changed – i.e. getting married, starting a family, others having influence etc. Should a situation present requiring them to go their separate ways, this could result in the brothers selling properties and paying exit costs and capital gains taxes or them needing to refinance, so Stewart could move forward independently, again potentially incurring cash and time costs. Neither option is ideal and could be avoided with planning.

In short, they had no exit strategy determined for different stages in their lives, leaving them vulnerable to problems down the track as personal circumstances changed and others potentially became involved in the mix (more regarding this in Step 3).

Another word of warning:
As per risk profiles, when investing, invest according to the person in the relationship with the lowest or most cautious risk appetite. If your risk profiles and appetites differ substantially then you may need to do some negotiating to find a solution you can both live with, but not at the expense of the less conservative of the two (if you want to stay together that is). Otherwise, go it alone. It is not uncommon to start a journey with an investment partner and then part ways or go independently when risk appetites and profiles differ substantially. If this isn't addressed UP FRONT however, it can cause problems down the track.

Other Factors to Consider

As an Accredited Property Investment Advisor, the other elements I consider when working with clients that form part of an investor's overall risk level when investing are their individual age(s), income, marital status, goals, number of dependents (children or otherwise), timeframe, borrowing capacity, debt levels, deposit size, qualification regarding government incentives (FHOG, NRAS), and personal preference for property types or strategies.

As a property investor, you should also take all of this into consideration when developing a property investment strategy. Not doing so could cause problems down the track that could have been avoidable.

Property and Strategy Risk – Understand property and strategy related types of risk

Aside from seeking out tailored advice, so many of the different property-related investment 'strategies' in the public are aligned with developers, property spruikers, wholesale distribution channels and selling agents. This can make knowing which way to go and what's right for you seem overwhelming.

Property Usage

Residential, Commercial, Industrial and Short Stay property types all have risk associated with their usage (zoning). For the purpose of simplicity and addressing the majority of individual property investors, this book will only delve into residentially zoned property in detail, as the others are quite complex in their own right and require a lot of specific and detailed information.

Strategy

Timeframes and Return

When deciding on a strategy that matches your risk profile, you also need to consider your goals and timeframes. Are they short-term or long-term and are they based on capital growth or cash flow?[2]

SHORT-TERM STRATEGIES

These are designed to generate cash flow or profit. These are usually higher risk as they depend upon market conditions behaving in a particular way at a particular time, so substantial due diligence is required in the local market and specific property knowledge. For the purpose of clarity, let's define short term as being less than five years.

---

2 As advised in the PIAA Property Investment Advice Course

The risk is reduced if you are buying at the beginning of an upward price movement in an area. This strategy requires strong technical knowledge, experience and funds to take quick action, and deal with unforeseen problems.

Examples of short-term strategies include developing, renovating, buying off the plan and 'flipping' before settlement, renovating and flipping, and buying property with lease options and selling the options. The type of property you buy for a short term strategy will also influence the amount of capital gain you could expect to make.

Case study – *Docklands, Melbourne Victoria*

There was a trend of buying apartments at the commencement of the development of the Docklands apartment precinct in 2000, which proved very profitable for many people who bought at the beginning of the rising market and exited along the way.

The downfall for many investors was when they bought based on the assumption that prices would keep increasing and without fully analysing the risk of who their next buyer might be, only to find they had purchased an apartment off the plan and not been able to resell (or flip for profit) before settlement, leaving themselves legally required to settle and developers taking legal action to recoup losses from those who couldn't. Worse still, it meant that some of the investors had to sell their principal home in the suburbs to fund the settlement of their investment property, resulting in whole families relocating and living in 2 bedroom apartments and then commuting many kilometres each day to take kids to back to the school in the zone where they used to live and were registered to attend.

Sadly these are often the investors who get burnt and think property is a bad investment. What they don't understand is that it was their lack of due diligence, research and understanding of risk that brought about their dilemma.

LONGER-TERM STRATEGIES

These are designed to generate capital growth and equity over time. These are often lower risk and, as a bonus, the investor has a longer time in the market to compensate for any buying mistakes that may be made from the outset. However, this is not always a guarantee of generating decent capital growth if the fundamentals around buying weren't right from the beginning. The long term prospects for the property should still be reviewed to determine if it is worthwhile holding onto for a longer period. (Refer to Step 7 for more information).

For the purpose of clarity, let's define long term as being 10 years or more.

These strategies are more beneficial the earlier you get into the market because as the property increases in value, so does the rent which can be used to eventually pay off the loans that may start from a place of negative gearing, become neutrally geared and then ultimately positively geared.

CAPITAL GROWTH STRATEGIES

Capital growth properties are those that are located in high-growth areas, where there is constant and increasing demand for accommodation, but where supply is limited.

An example of this is inner cities, where virtually all of the land has been developed and therefore no more properties can be built, unless you knock down a house and construct townhouses or units in its place.

Compound growth is an investor's best friend, which is why holding and not selling property as a strategy can be so effective. Leveraging to obtain equity growth over time will allow you, as an investor, to further leverage and build your portfolio.

This may be a good place to start if you are on a high income ($100,000 plus) and can benefit from negative gearing. Negative gearing is when the cost of owning the property (including mortgage interest, council rates, water rates, insurance and other expenses) is greater than the rental income that you receive, so you need to chip in money from your own pocket each month to cover the shortfall between the two. The shortfall can be claimed as a deduction against your income tax. This isn't necessarily a good starting strategy for investors earning less than $100,000 per annum, as they are in a relatively low tax bracket so the 'benefit' of negative gearing is limited.

You can see in the following chart, demonstrating the growth in value of a $400,000 property with varying rates of return over 30 years, that time in the market makes a huge difference. The longer you hold onto a property the better, due to the exponential growth in the later decades.

You can also see that a poor performing property at an average of just 3% growth per annum will cost you the owner millions of dollars of lost growth over a 30 year period, compared to a property with an average 8% growth per annum.

This highlights why research, selection and assessment of the asset is CRITICAL when creating wealth over the longer term (refer to Step 5).

PROPERTY PURCHASE PRICE $400,000				
Years	3%	5%	8%	11%
1	$412,000	$420,000	$432,000	$444,000
5	$463,710	$510,513	$587,731	$674,023
10	$537,567	$651,558	$863,570	$1,135,768
20	$722,444	$1,061,319	$1,854,383	$3,224,925
30	$970,905	$1,728,777	$4,025,063	$9,156,919

CASH-FLOW STRATEGIES

Positive cash flow properties generate more income for you each week than they cost you to maintain, making them the exact opposite of negatively geared properties. Positive cash flow properties are most often located in regional towns.

Also known as yield or rental income, these enable you to service debt and generate income, which can allow you to further leverage and continue to build your portfolio. This may be a good place to start if you are a lower income earner, especially if you receive no real benefit from negative gearing.

Some of these could include executive rentals, short stay/holiday rental of your property (subject to zoning), renting the property fully furnished, renting rooms out individually, buying in more affordable regional centres with strong tenant demand and low vacancy rates or buying in regional centres with strong demand and limited supply such as mining towns to create high returns (be wary of the additional risk factors).

COMBINED STRATEGIES

There are arguments for combining some or all of the strategies above, but they are dependent on your personal circumstances and of course factoring in your risk profiles and appetite, income, age, marital status, goals, etc.

ONE MORE THING

In addition to understanding your own risk profile and appetite, beware your ego in the investing process.

Sometimes, regardless of our intentions or how clever we think we are, we can get in our own way.

There are times when outsourcing is the best option, because we can't be an expert in everything and some things require more expertise than others (especially when investing hundreds of thousands of dollars).

An ego that's not in check can make rash decisions, but there's no point if you lose or don't make money as a result (e.g. developing to say you are a developer when really it's not compatible with your level of knowledge, the time that you can commit, the funds available or your risk profile).

KEY POINTS

- Understand your, and your partner's, personal risk profiles, risk attitudes, and risk appetites.

- Understand risk associated with different strategies/property types and invest accordingly.

- Invest so that you can sleep at night!

NOTES

STEP

Develop a
Strategy

3

Having learned about risk and having a better idea of your own and your partner's profiles and attitudes, as well as the risk associated with property types and various strategies, the next step is to put a plan into place and to take action!

Case Study – *Joe*

TIMEFRAMES

Joe wants to retire on $100,000 per annum in 20 years' time, which means, in today's dollars, he would need a net asset base of $2,000,000 earning approximately 5% per annum to generate the $100,000 per annum passive income.

This is, of course, subject to a lender allowing him to borrow at such a high loan to value ratio (LVR), most likely using cross-collateralisation, which can also be high risk and not recommended.

Note, net asset base means this is in addition to his own (unencumbered) home, as he will be living in it rather than deriving income from it. From here, he needs to work backwards to determine how many properties he needs to purchase, how frequently, at what price, earning what income and where and what to buy. This may be too complex for the average investor, which is why seeking independent advice may be beneficial.

RETIRE ON RENTS

Joe needs $2,000,000 worth of debt-free property to generate his $100,000 per annum, so he calculates that he needs to buy 5 properties averaging $400,000 each, earning 8% per annum average growth over a 10 year period. They appreciate to a value of $865,000 each and combined are worth $4,325,000. Joe needs to sell two of them to pay down his debts of $1,200,000 and pay capital gains tax, leaving him with his desired portfolio worth $2,595,000, which he can keep renting out to generate passive income.

REFINANCE INTO RETIREMENT

At its peak, Joe's portfolio is worth $4,325,000. He has debts of $1,200,000 so an LVR ratio of 27% i.e. 1,200,000/4,325,000 = 27 %. He could take out $100,000 to live off for the year and his new LVR would be 30%. This strategy may last him approximately 20 years even if his assets didn't increase at all for that time but by then he would have an LVR of 76% and may no longer have the capacity to draw down equity or pay the monthly mortgage repayments.

Timeframes and End Goals

You need to start with the end goal in mind, so that you can work backwards from there. To determine this you need to know your expenses and cost of living now (or the annual dollar amount you would to retire on in today's dollars) and you need to determine the size of the asset base required to generate this level of passive income. Ideally you will review this annually in conjunction with the value of your portfolio, to see if you are on target and so that you can modify your strategy as and when required and subject to circumstances at the time.

If you have a short timeframe that is potentially unrealistic, e.g. you want to retire in 10 years on $100,000 per annum and you don't currently own any property, the options are:

1   Ignore your risk profile and follow a strategy that is higher risk for a higher return to meet your short time frame (at the expense of not sleeping at night)

    OR

2   Readjust your expectations to a longer timeframe, especially if your income and means are limited.

It's always better to overestimate the income you will need and underestimate the return on the asset pool to allow a margin of safety.

In addition, as we live much longer nowadays, you may need to consider assets that will generate an income for 30 – 40 years, especially if you want to retire younger than the now standard 67 years of age.

Entry, Hold and Exit Strategies

Entry

This is your ability to enter the property investment market. You need to take into account your budget, cash flow, income, borrowing capacity, job stability and debt serviceability. This, in conjunction with your goals, will determine how to set up your strategy and how often you should review it along the way.

The main thing to take into consideration is to make sure that whatever path you go down, that you reduce risk! Always have income protection and a buffer of money to fall back on in the event of an emergency.

Hold

Most investors can buy something – the greater challenge lies with holding it until your goals have been achieved!

You must hold a property long enough to enable capital growth to develop, especially if you are looking at medium to long timeframes.

In shorter timeframes, you still need consider your ability to meet debt repayments whilst implementing your strategy.

Tricks such as fixing loans, having savings buffers, not biting off more than you can chew, having appropriate and multiple insurances in place, getting proper tax and accounting advice, reviewing rental returns regularly and maintaining your property will all contribute to your ability to hold over the short and long terms.

Other methods to assist holding over the long term include executive rentals, short stay/holiday rental of your property (subject to zoning), renting the property fully furnished or renting rooms out individually and at a premium compared to as a whole.

Knowing the available options if your situation changes is also really important, as selling property isn't always the best option in the first instance. These options may include refinancing your debt, taking a repayment holiday, changing to interest only if you haven't already financed on that basis, analysing your portfolio and selling properties that aren't performing at the level required to achieve your goals, earning a higher income, or tapping into your savings buffer.

Exit

There are three principal methods of exiting your property portfolio. Depending on how many properties you have bought, how old you are and how long you need to fund your retirement, these will influence the steps you take to exit your properties. These steps should be determined with your accountant, who can advise on tax and superannuation regulations and implications.

Your exit strategy will determine how many properties you may need, so to get the ball rolling select the one that appeals most to you.

RETIRE ON RENTS

This a simple 'vanilla' strategy that investors use to retire with via property ownership. Simply, the investor leverages into multiple properties over a period of time and at retirement, sells down the worst performing assets to pay off the debt and then lives off the rental income. All or most of the debt may be paid down, leaving the rental income to generate a passive income for the investor.

The number of properties required to follow this strategy needs to be determined based on the investor's individual circumstances. They could also create a mixed portfolio consisting of capital growth and yield properties.

Pros
- Rents and property values rise over time with inflation, or rent spikes based on high demand and limited supply

- Borrowings are reduced on retirement so there is little to no debt

Cons
- Still dealing with property managers and tenants in retirement

- Still need to maintain properties to an acceptable standard and maintain tenant appeal to maximise rent returns

- Changes to rent cycles and supply and demand factors can affect the level of income which can lead to income reductions as a result of periods of vacancy or the need to reduce rent

- Capital gains tax is payable upon the sale of the property at retirement. However, if you sought appropriate accounting advice before purchasing, the level of tax payable should have been minimised based on the advice received and actioned

REFINANCE INTO RETIREMENT

This is the riskiest approach . As per the 'retire on rents' strategy, the investor accumulates property, but instead of selling properties at retirement to pay down debt, the portfolio is refinanced in retirement so that the LVR is topped up periodically (i.e. the loan is drawn down further) to provide funds.

Effectively you are 'borrowing' money to pay for your living expenses and the danger of this is that there is no guarantee that the bank will continue to permit this on an ongoing basis, as the increased borrowings increase your debt repayments. The interest is capitalised, i.e. it's added to the principal, and when using debt for tax free living expenses, the interest payments are no longer deductible.

This strategy is also dependent upon ongoing capital growth to create equity that can be drawn against, and ongoing increases in rental income.

Pros
- Capital gains tax isn't payable because no property is sold

- Funds used to live off in retirement may not be taxed

Cons
- Relies on ongoing capital growth and rental increase to support the strategy

- Tenant responsibilities and property management requirements are retained

- A lender must be willing to allow such refinancing given debt serviceability will reduce over time

- Debt and interest obligations are carried into retirement

SELL UP AND REINVEST OR HOLD THE PROCEEDS

This strategy treats property investing as the vehicle to accumulate wealth to retire on, but not to derive ongoing passive income from.

By leveraging to accumulate property over time and then selling at retirement, the investor can then hold the proceeds in a low risk managed fund or annuity. This will provide ongoing passive income in the form of a distribution. The trade off at retirement, however, is that where you park your proceeds determines the income you will receive, and other forces can influence those returns, such as interest rates if you put it in a cash management trust.

To be successful in this method, you need to invest for high capital growth and allow adequate time for the portfolio to grow in value.

Remember the chart demonstrating the accumulating value of a $400,000 property? As you can see, the compounding growth from years 10 > 20 > 30 is substantial (especially at the higher returns), so the sooner you start investing, or the more time you have to hold your properties, the better financial result you are likely to generate upon exit.

YEAR 1 – PROPERTY PURCHASE PRICE $400,000				
Years	3%	5%	8%	11%
10	$537,567	$651,558	$863,570	$1,135,768
20	$722,444	$1,061,319	$1864,383	$3,224,925
30	$920,905	$1,728,777	$4,025,063	$9,156,919S

Pros
- No property management, tenant problems or ongoing property maintenance

- No debts or loan repayments at settlement

Cons
- Large capital gains tax bill incurred when portfolio is sold (remember – tax structuring must be done before purchase to ensure tax minimisation)

- Retirement income can fluctuate subject to market conditions and where you have parked your funds

MIX IT UP
Most investors will also receive some kind of payout from their compulsory superannuation fund at retirement.

This additional money could be used to pay off debt for options 1 or 2 or as an additional source of income to supplement the income from your property portfolio.

Note – as at the time of revision in 2016, no updated statistics were available from the ATO

INDIVIDUALS' RENTAL INCOME AND DEDUCTIONS, 2011-12 AND 2012-13 INCOME YEARS

Dividing the total rental income loss claimed by taxpayers by the number of taxpayers, reveals that the average loss recorded for negatively geared property investors was $10,947 in 2010-11, up from $9,132 in 2009-10.

	2011-12[1]		2012-13[1]	
Rental income/deductions	No.	$m	No.	$m
Gross rental income	1,873,210	34,000	1,944,080	36,593
Less rental interest deductions	1,532,300	24,178	1,591,610	22,548
Capital works deductions	798,075	2,167	857,975	2,440
Other rental deductions	1,880,845	15,531	1,952,530	16,998
Net rental income[2]	1,895,775	-7,860	1,967,260	-5,394

1 Data for the 2011-12 and 2012-13 income years includes data processed up to 31 October 2012 and 31 October 2013
2 Components do not add to the total number of taxpayers claiming rental deductions, because taxpayers may claim more than none type of deduction. Totals may differ from the sum of the components, due to rounding. Note – data is the most recent available at time of publication. (Source, ATO Taxation Statistics 2012 – 2013).

The figures show there was a small rise in gross rental income from $34 billion to $35.5 billion but a reduction in tax deductible rental interest payments (down from $24.1 billion to $22.5 billion), capital works deductions and other allowable rental deductions.

INDIVIDUALS' NET RENTAL INCOME, BY TAXABLE INCOME, 2010-11 INCOME YEAR[1]

The highest proportion of tax payers claiming rental deductions are those earning between $37,000 and $80,000 per year, making up more than a third of all negatively geared property investors.

What this reveals is that too many investors are on a relatively low income, and probably shouldn't be investing for 'negative gearing' benefits as they don't pay a lot of tax. They may actually be better off initially buying positively or neutrally geared property instead to increase or maintain their overall income, and therefore potentially increase their borrowing capacity, while ensuring they aren't so far out of pocket that their lifestyle is detrimentally affected.

Taxable Income	Net rental income less than $0		Net rental income, greater than or equal to $0			
	No.	$m	No.	$m	No.	Total $m
$6000 or less	110,322	-1,437	42,085	182	152,407	-1,255
$6001-$37,000	281,785	-2,521	222,437	1,711	504,222	-810
$37,001-$80,000	485,587	-4,605	195,645	1,676	681,232	-2,929
$80,001-$180,000	276,611	-3,311	109,664	1,235	386,275	-2,076
$180,001 or more	59,292	-1,412	27,746	620	87,038	-792
Total[2]	1,213,597	-13,285	597,577	5,423	1,811,174	-7,862

1 Data for the 2010-11 income year includes data processed up to 31 October 2012
2 Totals may differ from the sum of the components, due to rounding

Remember, things such as depreciation, negative gearing and NRAS benefits are a BENEFIT of investing and shouldn't be the underlying DRIVER to purchase a property.

Case Study - *John*

John had attended a seminar with a 'wealth creation group' where he was introduced to the concept of 'negative gearing'. He then attended a personal 'strategy' session with a 'property advisor' (selling agent) where he was offered two off the plan house and land packages. He borrowed 90% plus costs for each $500,000 property at 6% interest. They each returned $400 per week rent.

Allowing for the properties' incomes, expenses, his loan repayments, depreciation benefits and John's taxable income, every week he was out of pocket by $376 NET after tax ($188 per property), and $404 before tax ($202 per week per property) or $19,552 per annum.

As you can see, his tax benefit was only $28 a week, or $1456 per annum – not much at all for the $900,000 worth of debt and substantial risk he had taken on board. In addition, the properties' growth to date hasn't been great and their location doesn't have enough of the necessary growth drivers to provide him with above average capital growth long term. Given his situation as the sole bread winner for his young family, he would have been better off starting with one neutrally to positively geared yield property, and then reviewing his position to assess what the next property should be (capital growth or yield) and how it should be structured and geared.

Budgeting and Personal Cash Flow

Before purchasing property you need to have 12 months of your income personally assessed, including all of your out-going expenses to determine your personal cash flow situation. Understanding how much weekly disposable income you have available to allocate to property investment and when and how often your largest financial commitments fall throughout the year, is your starting point.

Remember to budget money for emergency, unexpected extras, holidays, special occasions and also take into account all the insurances you will need to purchase when increasing debt.

By doing this you can allocate funds and manage money as required (even if you have to set up extra bank accounts to channel money into).

Timing into and Out of Markets

One can argue that timing into a market is where you make money. While this can be correct and may be a primary driver when working to short-term timeframes or strategies, you need to do a lot of analysis and research and at the end of the day, even the experts who work in property research full time don't always get it right.

Sometimes it's more about just getting into and spending time IN the market rather than timing the market, however if the herd is being carried along and prices are escalating madly, it may be a good time to sit back and watch while investigating other opportunities that aren't so hot. When they zig, you zag!

Fortune also favours the brave, but NOT at the expense of due diligence. I wish I could tell you that you can make money in property with no effort, no money down and no need for due diligence or risk mitigation, alas that's not how it works!

When is the best time to invest? You can try and monitor market conditions based on the diagram below, but there are markets within markets and they can and do perform independently of the cycle below. Even the property experts who commentate on the market can have differing viewpoints.

At a minimum, invest when you can afford to and when the banks will lend you money. Both of these situations can change quickly (remember the clamp down on lending when the GFC hit) and when APRA changes to lending policy slowed down the heated market in 2015. Don't always assume you will qualify for funds when you want them! Importantly, by doing your due diligence wisely and over the long term, paying market price or close to it shouldn't have too big an impact in the longer term.

Getting out of the market towards retirement should start to be considered approximately 5 years out from your target retirement date. As property isn't liquid you may need extra time up your sleeve to dispose of it.

In addition, other market factors relating to other asset types within your superfund can also influence your transition into retirement, so these should also be taken into account with the expert advisors that you engage.

PROPERTY CLOCK

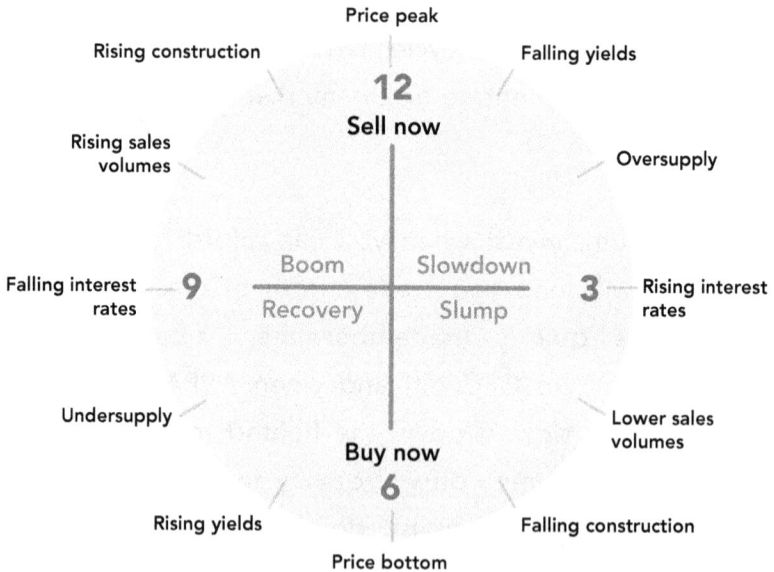

KEY POINTS

- Start with your end goal in mind and work backwards from there.

- Work to realistic timeframes.

- Determine your entry, hold and exit strategy before purchasing (they can change and be reviewed over time).

- What fears are preventing you from moving forward and what do you need to do about it to eliminate them?

- Consider balancing your portfolio. Negative gearing isn't suitable for everyone, ESPECIALLY if you are on an income of less than $80,000 per annum!

- Assess your budget and cash flow so you can determine your disposable income and allocate funds accordingly.

- Get into the market when you can afford to and when the banks will lend you the money.

NOTES

STEP

Engage Your Team of Experts

4

Australians love property! As a topic of conversation, it is something that many of us have in common and we love talking about it. Whether it's our latest buy, a course we are doing, or a seminar we attended, we frequently share ideas, concepts, experiences and strategies.

The danger here lies in the fact that there are so many steps involved in the property research, analysis and buying process that being too simplistic in your approach can result in problems that cost thousands.

Just as most people wouldn't seek advice from friends about heart surgery or mechanical repairs on their car (at least, not if they weren't a mechanic), it's important to realise that the same level of awareness should apply when investing hundreds of thousands on property. By all means, have the conversation with friends or family and do the networking but, as everyone's personal circumstances are different, always seek the opinion of independent experts before acting on information or 'advice' given in good faith. One size often doesn't fit all, and if you try to make it, it can result in all sorts of problems!

Why Engage Experts

Ask yourself a question. How much of your investment returns (capital growth or rental returns) would you like to maximise, keep and not pay in tax, and how much would you like to reduce your risk? If your answer is as much as possible, then it's **imperative** that you consider engaging most, if not all, of the following experts.

Think of property investing as a **property business**, and these experts all form part of the success of that business. Independently they help you to maximise the investment opportunity and/or minimise risk, while collectively they combine to increase your success multi-fold.

Do you think Warren Buffet or Kerry Packer achieved their level of success without engaging experts to support and guide them along the way? Of course not, and the same applies when you're building your property portfolio.

If you were building a house, the expert advice referred to below is equal in importance to the concrete, frame, bricks and mortar, which form the structure and foundations of the building. There could be significant financial consequences if you discovered the concrete was too thin and the mortar too weak AFTER the house had been built!

The same applies with engaging experts to help you in the property investing process. After you have purchased the property, it's often too late for these experts to be able to help you (with the exception of the quantity surveyor).

Conversely, following the steps below in the order presented will enable you to invest in property sustainably and prosperously.

ENGAGING EXPERTS

YOU

1st

Before doing anything...
◄ Accredited Property Investment Advisor and/or Buyer Agent
◄ Accountant/Financial Planner
◄ Mortgage Broker

2nd

Before signing a conditional or unconditional contract...
◄ Solicitor/Conveyancer
◄ Licensed Valuer

3rd

Once a conditional contract is signed or before bidding at auction...
◄ Building Inspector
◄ Pest Inspector

4th

Once the contract becomes unconditional...
◄ Property Manager
◄ Insurance Broker

5th

After your property has settled...
◄ Quantity Surveyor

FIGURE 1

As you can see in the previous diagram, there are usually ten professions that touch a property purchasing transaction and they all provide a very important role. Like all industries, you need to be able to source the best, choosing experts that specialise in working with property investors who are building a portfolio over time. Why? Because they need to step into the future with you and consider the implications of how big you want to build your portfolio, what type of properties you will buy, which strategies you will use, who will benefit financially and when. This information empowers them to provide the correct advice, planning and structuring in advance. Why in advance? Because getting into a bad property investment is much easier than getting OUT of one!

Begin at the Beginning

Different experts need to be engaged along the way, and some need to be engaged simultaneously.

First Stage
ACCREDITED PROPERTY INVESTMENT ADVISOR
AND/OR BUYER AGENT.

An Accredited Property Investment Advisor (APIA) is a member of the Property Investment Association of Australia (PIAA). An APIA is a fully Licensed Estate agent who has voluntarily done additional studies (including a number of financial planning subjects and an accreditation course) to enable them to use that title, act in that capacity and qualify for professional indemnity insurance as an Accredited Property Investment Advisor (which is a rarity in the industry).

You could say that an APIA is an early adopter of a model and standard of how 'property advisors' should consult with their clients, and is operating to a standard and industry benchmark that hasn't yet formally been created, in spite of the desperate need for it.

An APIA works for the client on a fee for service basis to determine and analyse their property goals and model scenarios to determine a suitable strategy based on their needs and goals – taking into account timeframes to achieve the goals; entry, hold and exit considerations; borrowing capacity; risk profiles and appetite; age(s); income; marital status; goals; number of dependents (children or otherwise); debt levels; deposit size; qualification for government incentives (first home owners grant, NRAS) and personal preference for property types or strategies.

They then develop a Statement of Property Investment Advice (SOPIA) which supports the client's best interests and assists in the acquisition of property over time to fulfil that strategy. Professional standards and a code of conduct are adhered to and transparency is expected of all advisors.

The provision of a SOPIA from an APIA could also enable the investor to approach a commercial lender from the viewpoint that the SOPIA confirms the strategy/plan that the property business is based upon. This opens up all sorts of beneficial possibilities for the investor, including potential access to much more competitive commercial lending interest rates and loan structuring.

As per figure 1, they can also provide the role of coordinating and liaising with all parties that touch the property transaction, such as your accountant, mortgage broker, solicitor, building and pest inspectors and possibly the property manager. This ensures that the 'left hand' knows what the 'right hand' is doing and that all experts are on the same page and communicating.

Importantly, an APIA (unlike other 'property advisors') will have professional indemnity insurance that covers them for the provision of 'property investment advice'.

Client Case Study – *Jessica*

Jessica engaged our services to develop a long-term strategy, so she could achieve her goal of retiring and living off the passive income from her property portfolio within a 16 year timeframe.

Whilst she was an experienced investor, she was sold an investment property that was performing poorly and recognised the value in sourcing independent advice. She wanted to continue to grow her property portfolio, but having had a negative experience with her first investment property, she wasn't sure what to do to advance her position or how to fix the negative equity trap she found herself in.

She had no strategy, no clear and specific goal, no understanding of her risk profile and the limitation of her age, no clarity about where to invest and why and was distrusting of people representing themselves as property experts.

After taking into consideration her existing property portfolio, age, goals, income, marital status, risk profile, risk appetite, borrowing capacity and timeframe, we developed a tailored strategy and a Statement of Property Investment Advice (SOPIA).

In addition to the strategy, a property solution was provided, taking into account the macro and micro economic indicators that influence property growth – local factors including employment and economic growth, population and demographic changes, infrastructure, government spending and supply and demand factors.

Buyer Agent

Just as a solicitor can act/work for the defendant or the plaintiff/prosecution in a legal matter, a Licensed Estate Agent can act/work for the buyer or the vendor in a property transaction, but never both at the same time.

When explaining what I do to people, I use the analogy that **'asking a selling agent for advice when buying property is like going to court to fight criminal charges, but without engaging a solicitor to defend you, and then also asking the prosecutor for advice'**.

A buyer agent's (or buyer advocate's) principal role is to research, source and negotiate to buy property on your behalf. They legally act for and represent the interests of the buyer. They advocate on your behalf as a fee for service professional, effectively creating a protective barrier between you and the selling agent or vendor.

While you may only ever buy property once or twice, a buyer agent is in the market researching and negotiating every day, so their skills are well-honed and they have access to the same professional and industry databases which selling agents use, but are not readily available to the general public. They understand the tactics selling agents use to sell property and are able to source properties that are 'pre or off market' before the general public find out about them, due to the established relationships they have with selling agents.

While many are often experienced in buying 'owner occupier' style property for clients, this doesn't automatically make them all experts at what constitutes an investment grade property, so you need to do your research.

And be aware! In some states there is no formal definition under the Real Estate Act that defines the term 'buyer agent', therefore the term can be subject to being misused, albeit that could be deemed misleading and deceptive conduct by Consumer Affairs.

Check with your local Real Estate Institute regarding who can call themselves a 'buyer's agent' or 'buyer advocate' and be aware that in many states, there are selling agents that also act as buyer agents for clients at times.

For the purpose of this book, I define a buyer agent as follows:

- They are always an agent's representative working for a Licensed Estate Agent, or are a Licensed Estate Agent themselves. They are a single focus agency who don't also sell property and beware of those who are unlicensed.

- They are ideally a member of their state-based Real Estate Institute and attend and meet their continuing professional development (CPD) requirements. In some states membership is not compulsory.

- They buy established property and generally don't encourage you to buy brand new or off the plan property for investment purposes. The only exception would be if you brief them that that's what you want to live or invest in, or circumstances dictate new or off the plan (such as a foreign investor client), however they should also provide information on the pros and cons of this investment strategy.

- They have professional indemnity insurance which covers them in their role as a Licensed Estate Agent (only).

- They work in the established market and source property via general selling/real estate agents or off market (i.e. they don't present you with developer stock, new developments or off the plan property).

- They provide written reports and market evidence to substantiate their recommendations.

- They should be able to buy for you city-wide and a select few will also have regional expertise. Conversely, if they only buy in limited select suburbs or geographical areas, they can't always work within your budget. Seek to engage a buyer advocate who can work with you if your budget is very low and who isn't limited to only a small geographic area.

Ideally they are also an APIA or a formally qualified property investment advisor, as they will have a much broader understanding of the factors that affect property growth, a much higher skill set and stronger expertise regarding property investing, so will therefore be able to provide more specialised advice.

In addition, they are a fulltime buyer agent. i.e they don't work mostly as a selling agent and then do the 'occasional' buyer advocacy deal. These agents often don't fully represent their buyers interests, as their mindset is mostly 'vendor' focused. I personally feel that you can only excel at your role and advocate for your client if you are fully committed to the buyer (or vendor) and focus on that 'side of the fence' 95-100% of the time.

Note:

- Some buyer agents may have a property management division, but make sure you also check what their competition are offering so you can make an informed decision as to who you engage and why (refer below to Fourth Stage – Property Manager).

- Some buyer agents may offer vendor advocacy where they support and advise the vendor during the sale of a property, whereas others may specialise in buyer advocacy only.

Never deal with anyone acting as or calling themselves a buyer agent who doesn't have formal real estate qualifications, otherwise they are operating outside Real Estate Law, which means they legally can't charge you/ take money from you if representing you in a real estate transaction AND they won't be covered by professional indemnity insurance if things go wrong.

Also, if they charge you an upfront fee and then have it reimbursed back to you once you have purchased a property, this means they are probably acting for the vendor as a selling agent and NOT acting in your interests as a buyer agent, so beware!

WHAT DOES A BUYER AGENT DO?

Their service offering can range from providing a full service where they research the market, source and find the property and negotiate the purchase on your behalf (representing you at auction bidding or by private treaty), to only negotiating the purchase price, clauses and terms in your favour, after you have found the property yourself.

Some buyer agents focus on working with home buyer/ owner occupier clients only while others specialise purely on investor clients and some provide a general service to both. They charge either a flat fee or a percentage of the sale price of a property (like a selling agent). While some may argue that you can do it yourself and a buyer agent costs too much, what a skilled buyer agent can achieve in terms of access to pre or off market property, price, terms and negotiated extras far outweighs the fee.

An (investment specialist) buyer agent is well worth the fee they charge, as they will not only protect you from making a costly mistake, but will save time and stress, while acquiring investment-grade properties which have the criteria to outperform the average over the long term, resulting in you ultimately earning thousands of dollars more.

A highly skilled and experienced (investment specialist) buyer agent with additional formal property investment advice qualifications will:

- Do a needs analysis for you, and understand your risk profile,

- Eliminate most of property for sale in the marketplace from consideration,

- Provide a documented investment strategy,

- Provide financial modelling and evidence based reporting to substantiate any recommendations presented to you, and

- Provide you with guidance when engaging a property manager.

Generally speaking, there are selling agents who appreciate working with buyer agent's and have nurtured professional relationships, as they bring qualified buyers to the table, can facilitate 'off market' deals and make the post-sale process easier.

There are also some selling agents who 'dumb down' a buyer agent's service offering by perpetuating the myth of fees being too high or by declaring that buyer agents are 'failed selling agents' (this is absolute rubbish – if they failed at selling they would definitely fail at buying given the skill set is far more demanding).

In reality, when selling agents have to deal with a professional and experienced buyer agent and negotiator on the other side of a deal, it can actually make their job much harder than dealing with an inexperienced or naïve buyer, hence any negative spin and commentary from them.

Having worked as a Licensed Estate Agent - working both for vendors/sellers and buyers - for a number of years in each capacity and in two different states of Australia, I can personally attest to the fact that dollar for dollar, a highly experienced (investment specialist) buyer agent provides a much broader and more valuable service for their fee than a selling agent.

Before you spend (risk) hundreds of thousands of dollars buying property, I would encourage you as an investor or home buyer to meet with a buyer agent to gain a better understanding of how they can help you, so that you make a fully informed decision as to whether to use their services or not.

Note:
- As a home buyer, it is still very important that you buy well from an investment perspective, as you will likely rely on the growth of your property to leverage against in the future, thus allowing you to continue to invest to create wealth.

Client Case Study – *Miranda*

A client re-engaged our services to buy an owner-occupier property, in a very small, tightly held and popular suburb in Melbourne, with a very specific budget.

Miranda was an experienced investor and understood the importance of her home needing to have good underlying capital growth that she could leverage later on, while also meeting her needs as a home owner. She was clear and specific in her requirements and her brief and she also preferred not to buy at auction. It needed to be a particular price point, suburb and age but there was flexibility around timeframes.

After searching the small suburb in which there was little to no stock available for sale, we were able to source a property off market (i.e. it wasn't promoted for sale to the general public) and negotiate directly with the vendor. Dealing with the vendor (an experienced property developer), we were able to negotiate to buy the property $50,000 below bank valuation, while inserting clauses to protect our client and to negotiate a satisfactory outcome that suited both parties, very quickly and easily for all.

In addition, the settlement was unintentionally delayed by the vendor, so we negotiated for Miranda to move in before settlement with a secure legal agreement in place that everyone was happy with, including the vendor's solicitor. Miranda saved thousands by not having to live in a hotel for weeks and move her belongings into and out of storage in that time.

This was a fantastic result on many levels and couldn't have been achieved without the expertise of a highly skilled Buyer Agent (this case study continues under Building and Pest Inspector below).

Accountant

The investment conversation may initiate with your accountant and then progress to meeting with an APIA or buyer agent, or it could start with your APIA or buyer agent and you could be referred back to your accountant for advice.

Your accountant isn't generally able to provide you with individual property advice as they are not knowledgeable in this area. However they CAN and SHOULD provide you with the tax and cash-flow guidance that you need to make an informed decision on your property strategy.

Ideally your accountant should be highly knowledgeable in property taxation matters, and will be proactive in helping you to meet your goals (rather than reactive to your situation). They will assist you with all the compliance requirements of lodging your tax return on an ongoing basis and advise on keeping accurate records, which will contribute to the success of your property business.

More importantly they will help and advise you (before you purchase the property) as to the most appropriate structure/entity in which to purchase it based on your personal, business and family circumstances, taking into account income minimisation and risk mitigation in conjunction with your overall Financial Plan. Why endeavour to create wealth if you are going to give it back to the ATO because you didn't seek the correct advice BEFORE purchasing a property?

It is imperative that you know your strategy before purchasing and have advice from your accountant as to what name to purchase the property in so that you are properly set up from the beginning. To see your accountant AFTER the purchase is too late, because they may not be able to help you at that stage. Also the option of adding the phrase 'and/or nominee' to the contract of sale has different stamp duty implications in different states. For example, adding the phrase in Victoria often allows a transfer of the title at settlement without incurring a double stamp duty payment whereas in Western Australia, this type of 'strategy' of buy now and sort it out later can result in stamp duty being paid twice as the State Revenue Office/Office of State Revenue (OOSR) regulations are different between the states. This could also apply in other states and policy regarding legislation can change frequently, so you need to check this every time with a solicitor or conveyancer in THAT state - who will know the rules specific to the property you are proposing to purchase!

Finally, you can't amend a contract of sale after the signing even if both parties agree, as this could be deemed an attempt to avoid paying stamp duty, and may result in penalties or double stamp duty regardless.

Land tax obligations also differ from state to state, so ensure you seek advice regarding ownership structures before buying outside of the state you live in.

Case Study – *Jason and Elizabeth*

Jason and Elizabeth took the view that due to potential negative gearing benefits, they should purchase the property in the name of the highest income earner. The problem with this was that after a few years the property became positively geared, therefore as Elizabeth was the higher income earner, she ended up paying tax at the highest marginal rate on the rental income.

Worst of all, if they sold the property, the Capital Gain from the property would also be taxed at the highest rate.

When you consider that high performing investment grade properties can double in price in seven to 10 years, you may lose much of the gain in taxes due to the apparent 'benefit' of negative gearing from the commencement.

If it is deemed required, most accountants can refer you to a financial planner, or they may have an in-house financial planner you can access.

You need to understand the difference between your accountant (who is allowed to give you advice on tax structures and options, as you would expect) and a financial planner, who is not generally allowed to give tax advice unless they have an additional qualification. i.e. you need to be sure that you are asking the right questions of the right professional.

Financial Planner
Since July 1st 2013, financial planners have been required to support self-directed clients (those who know what they want to invest in before their consultation) with good quality property investment advice. If they do not have specific qualifications or expertise in this area or are not permitted under their financial planning license to provide direct/real property advice, they are required to refer the client to a suitable expert (such as an Accredited Property Investment Advisor or Buyer Agent), or send the client away.

In most cases financial planners are like general practitioners – they provide an overview of your situation. It's important to understand and know what your overall goals are in conjunction with a cash-flow analysis, risk profile analysis, superannuation, and SMSF (self-managed Super Fund) structuring, and ensure you have the correct insurance levels to protect your family should anything go wrong. Once the overall plan and asset allocations are agreed to (sometimes it doesn't include a direct property allocation so you need to instruct them that this is what you want), it is vital to engage the respective experts in different areas to assist with implementing the overall plan. If you don't engage a financial planner to assist with overall planning, they can assist you with your insurance requirements as you increase your investment debt.

Also your financial planner isn't generally able to provide you with individual property advice as they are not licensed or knowledgeable in this area. However, like an accountant, they CAN and SHOULD provide you with the cash-flow guidance that you need to make an informed decision on your property strategy.

Ideally you will have access to a financial planner who also has accounting and tax qualifications, so that they are able to speak and advise you in a more complete manner.

Mortgage Broker
Choosing the right loan is vital when investing in property, refinancing your home or buying your own home.

Mortgage brokers are independent which means they aren't aligned to a single lender and they have the ability to search the market across dozens of lenders and hundreds of products to match the right product and rate to your needs as a property investor. They will save you time and money; however, it's not just about the interest rate, as there are other factors to take into consideration.

They should have substantial experience working with property investors who own large portfolios and will therefore know ahead of time what considerations need to be taken into account when approaching banks for funds on your behalf. They will save you time and they also know how to present an application to a lender (so that you have the best possible chance of getting the finance approved). Remember, you don't know what you don't know about dealing with lenders, but a mortgage broker does!

They will also work to mitigate risk and will structure the loans appropriately, as they will seek to understand what your investment plans are for both now and the future, and they can liaise directly with you accountant or financial planner as required.

Dealing with a bank directly will result in the bank selling you their product range and they generally won't provide detailed explanations about loan structuring, often because they haven't been trained to do so. In short, the advice won't be independent, because they only have their suite of products to sell.

Mortgage brokers can also assist if you are self-employed or have had a bad credit rating. Don't be afraid to pay them a fee for their expertise, because some of them can create finance miracles that you as an individual would never be able to achieve on your own.

Case Study – *Sarah*

Sarah met with her banker to ask about what cheap interest rates and investment loan products she could qualify for. Her banker was very helpful and preapproval came through quite quickly. He didn't however talk with her about her short-, medium-, or long-term investment goals – he simply provided her with a short-term solution based on her request. Sarah purchased her property and everything went to settlement quite smoothly.

After 18 months, Sarah was ready to reinvest again and after speaking to a mortgage broker this time to secure another stand-alone loan, she received some shocking news. Because her loan hadn't been set up to take into account further purchases, it meant she had to refinance into a different loan product to allow for structuring for growth. While this in itself wasn't too bad, because she fixed the rate on 100% of her loan for 3 years, it meant that she would incur an $11,780 break free to refinance and access her equity for her next purchase. Her choices were to pay the $11,780 or wait until the end of the fixed period of her loan. If she paid the fee, she would be out of pocket and if she waited, she would be 18 months behind in her investing, which could cost her a lot more if the market increased during that time!

Had Sarah received the correct and specialised advice on portfolio structuring from the very beginning, she wouldn't have had the costly lesson of incurring break costs to access her equity to continue to invest.

Be aware that many accountants, financial planners, lenders and mortgage brokers earn substantial commissions/marketing fees by referring clients to property spruikers/project marketers (Refer to Appendix 1 to learn more about this process).

If the calibre and quality of the property offering is poor, there can be substantial negative financial consequences to investors when taking up these referrals and buying the property recommended by these groups. While the referrer will earn thousands of dollars, the investor could lose thousands of dollars by buying poorly!

Second Stage
SOLICITOR/CONVEYANCER/SETTLEMENT AGENT

In law, conveyancing is the transfer of a property title from one person to another.

When purchasing a property a conveyancer can be employed prior to signing a contract (recommended) to reduce your risk of biased special conditions and to make enquiries (or review) the title, easements, outgoings, planning restrictions and notices affecting the property.

Once you and the seller of the property have signed the contract, a conveyancer's responsibility is to thoroughly search the title and Government authorities (e.g. council, water, land tax, building approvals, etc.) to provide you information about the property you are buying, and to arrange all the necessary documentation to ensure stamp duty can be paid and the transfer of the property can be lodged at the local Titles Office.

The conveyancer coordinates and attends settlement with all the parties (typically four including the purchaser and vendor's conveyancer and the purchaser and vendor's banks). They calculate the amount of outgoings (and income where the property is tenanted) and apportion them between the parties as well as ensuring any debts owed to any authority are paid at settlement. Ask your conveyancer to explain Title insurance to you and buy it for older properties that have been renovated or modified, if it is available in your State.

Once settlement is complete they will ensure the authorities are notified of the change of ownership.

If you are dealing with a solicitor it is also important to address the issue of updating your Will, or at an absolute minimum, getting one done if you don't already have one. There's no point creating wealth and then upon passing, leaving it to the State to determine the outcome for your relatives simply because you haven't drafted a Will.

Case Study – *Charlene and Mark*

Charlene and Mark were buying their first home. Their offer was accepted subject to finance and terms were agreed. After signing the contracts, they found a settlement agent (in WA) and had them go through the contract.

What came to light was that there was a caveat lodged against the property by a bank and the vendor had to meet certain obligations before the bank would release the caveat and allow the transfer of title (settlement) take place.

As Charlene and Mark lived in a state where there was no 'cooling off' period, they had nowhere to go other than to accept and wait for an outcome. The problem was that they were renting and based on the settlement terms in the contract, they had already given notice that they were vacating their rented home and worse, it had been let to another party very quickly.

Leading up to their moving date, they were made aware that settlement wouldn't take place on the agreed date and no one could answer when it would take place because the situation was beyond their control. They needed to find somewhere to live and fast!

In the end, they rented short stay holiday accommodation from month to month at a financial premium. They learned the hard way to always get a contract checked before signing anything.

Had they done that, they may have been able to negotiate a more suitable outcome under the circumstances and saved thousands of dollars on additional rental costs

LICENSED VALUER

A licensed valuer is a person who, by education, training and experience, is qualified to perform a property valuation. Also known as a 'sworn valuer', they hold a certified practising valuer's certificate and are recognised at law to be a property valuation professional who is charged with responsibility to be fair minded and transparent in their decision-making process.

By comparison, a real estate agent appraisal or bank valuation does not have legal recognition. An estate agent can only provide an 'appraisal' of value. A bank (mortgage) valuation, on the other hand, is specifically done for financial purposes and may not necessarily reflect true market conditions. Bank valuations have a reputation for being on the conservative side, based mostly on risk analysis and lending practice relevant to the specific lender or bank.

A good certified practising valuer can assist in the risk mitigation process and is qualified to provide objective and independent advice regarding the value of a property based on recent past sales evidence and other factors. They will not only look at past sales relevant to the property being valued, but also drill down on features associated with the property such as: location, style of construction, quality of the fit out, condition, size and age of the improvements. In addition to market supply and demand variables, they will also overlay their analysis with current market conditions, such as whether the market is bullish or soft.

Engaging a licensed valuer is very useful when selling a property, as they can protect vulnerable vendors from estate agents who over quote sale prices to secure the listing. Importantly, they can also assist in confidentially setting a realistic reserve price prior to an auction. If purchase interest is shown above the valuation provided by the property valuer, then the report doesn't need to be revealed, however, if buyer interest is below that valuation figure, the vendor would be in a position to defend the higher reserve using the valuation report.

For an investor, engaging a valuer is an option worth considering if they lack skill or confidence in appraising property prices, but not essential.

Client case study: *Rose and Dan*

Rose and Dan were about to buy their first investment property. Nervous about their budget, they engaged a valuer to help them determine their purchase limit. The valuation for the property came in at $700,000 with $35,000 leeway to factor in any competitive bidding on the day.

The property selected was a high-demand and low-supply unrenovated property in one of the four most desired streets in the suburb. The bidding started at $700,000 and stopped at $865,000, with five parties involved in driving up the price. In this instance, competition driven by emotion and development potential escalated the bidding so much.

Rose and Dan missed out and, two years later, that property now looks like it was good buying (in hindsight). Of course, because the market could have turned the other way a bank valuer wouldn't have agreed with the price at the time of purchase.

Third Stage
BUILDING INSPECTOR
A building inspector is an experienced and qualified registered builder who should be trained in accordance with the Australian Inspection Standard.

They will come and inspect and report on the structural, plumbing and maintenance elements of the property and provide a report and detailed analysis of the condition of the property in an easy to read format. The quality of the inspection can vary widely in terms of what is reviewed and how it is reported so shop around.

There are also experienced and qualified registered builders that specialise in rectification works, so they can inspect a property with evident structural damage and report on the extent of that damage and approximate costs to repair.

As you are spending hundreds of thousands of dollars, it would be negligent for you to skip this step, even if you have a high risk profile. It is worthwhile paying for a more expansive inspection if the property is older or has been renovated.

Client Case Study – *Miranda*

Back to Miranda (see Buyer Agent). During the course of the due diligence period that we negotiated into her contract, it came to light that there were substantial structural rectification repairs required on the property, even though it was only 10 years old. We knew there were issues before the inspections, but the subsequent building quote, based on

---

obtaining a specialist building inspection report, identified $35,000 – $50,000 worth of repairs needing to be done.

Miranda could have walked away at that point, however as she loved the property, (and only because of the specialised clauses we negotiated earlier into the contract on her behalf), we were able to renegotiate a substantial rebate at settlement that paid for the repairs to be completed.

This gave Miranda the freedom to select and engage a builder of her choice and in her own timeframe. In addition, and only because of the specialised clauses used, a number of smaller repairs worth approximately $3,000 were also attended to and paid for by the vendor before settlement. Again, this was to the satisfaction all parties and the property proceeded to settlement without a hitch.

This was a fantastic result on many levels and couldn't have been achieved without the expertise of a highly skilled Buyer Agent being involved in the process. The initial building inspection report only cost her $600. A worthwhile investment!

At the same time the building inspector attended the property, Miranda engaged a pest inspector to also attend. In this case there was a tree in the courtyard that was of concern. The pest inspection resulted in the report identifying that the tree had previous borer activity and was dead. It needed to be and consequently was removed to ensure that the borers were removed from proximity to the property and therefore eliminated the risk of future damage to the property.

The pest inspection report cost her $195. Another worthwhile investment!

PEST INSPECTOR

A pest inspector is a licensed, trained and fully insured inspector who will come and inspect and report on the level of pest activity in the house you are purchasing. The quality of the inspection can vary widely in terms of what is reviewed and how it is reported.

The reporting should include commentary regarding areas of live or past pest activity and the level of resulting damage, if any. It should also determine if there are conditions conducive to ongoing or potential damage and so should report ways to minimise the risk of pest activity as well as report if there are existing pest management systems in place.

As you are spending hundreds of thousands you should never skip this step! It is also worthwhile paying for a more expansive inspection if the property is older or has been renovated. This will often include photographs which are extremely helpful when it comes to getting quotes should there be any repairs required that you need to consider BEFORE buying the property (unconditionally).

COMBINED

There are inspectors that do a combination of building and pest inspections. The pest component may not be as comprehensive as an independent inspector in each instance, but ask questions and get clear around what they do and what they don't provide before choosing to go ahead.

Fourth Stage
PROPERTY MANAGER

Once you have an unconditional contract of sale you need to consider who to engage to manage your property. Unless you have done a state based Real Estate Institute course on property management to learn and understand all of your legal obligations as a landlord and the rights of the tenant, you should be paying a professional to manage it for you. Managing a property may seem easy, but rest assured it isn't and when it turns bad, it's often too late to engage someone to clean up the mess (and that's really when you need help!).

An astute property manager will mitigate risk on your behalf from the very beginning by vetting prospective tenants – checking them against industry databases of bad tenants and checking references.

At a minimum:
- They are always an Agent's Representative or fully Licensed Estate Agent

- They are a member of the state/local Real Estate Institute

- Their employer has professional indemnity insurance which covers them acting in their role as a Licensed Estate Agent or Agent's Representative

- Their ratio of property managers/support staff to properties under management does not exceed more than 120 properties in their portfolio, otherwise all they do is put out fires and deal with disgruntled tenants and landlords, while your property doesn't actually get 'managed' on your behalf

- They inspect your property a minimum of two times per annum (the wrong tenant can do a lot of damage in 12 months) and provide you with a detailed documented report including pictures for each inspection

- They don't have a high turnover of property managers and provide adequate and ongoing training and professional development for their staff

- Ideally they also own investment property themselves and have a good understanding of what a landlords needs and expectations are when managing their asset, often worth hundreds of thousands

Case Study – *Melanie*

Melanie decided to self-manage her property, thinking it was easy.

Her tenant complained that her air-conditioning unit was broken. Melanie told her tenant that she couldn't afford to repair or replace it, but offered her a $10 per week rental decrease to compensate for the lack of cooling. The tenant agreed but the law states that you can't do that. Legally, it has to be fixed and you cannot override legislation with a personal agreement. Unfortunately Melanie didn't know this.

A claim was later lodged with the local tenancy tribunal. It turns out that the tenant wasn't happy with the situation and had applied for a rent reduction of $30 per week for the two-and-a-half years that the air-conditioning wasn't fixed – plus the costs of living in a motel room during the really hot months, as she couldn't cope without cooling. In total, the tenant was asking for around $10,000.

As it's illegal for a landlord to fail to repair something like this, the tenancy tribunal found in favour of the tenant and the money was paid out of Melanie's pocket to the tenant. By attempting to save approximately $1500 a year in property management fees, it cost Melanie $10,000. Ouch!

INSURANCE BROKER

An insurance broker is similar to an accountant or lawyer who provides impartial professional advice, based on years of training, education and experience.

A professional insurance broker deals with many insurers and has access to different types of policy wordings. They act for their clients and help them to decide what risks to insure, what types of cover are best and how much it should cost. They can also consider if there are other ways that the risk can be transferred such as self-insuring and other non-traditional insurance products. In many cases the insurance broker is most valuable in the event of a claim. Until recently, insurance brokers learnt their trade through practical experience. However, now there are dedicated tertiary courses and continuing professional development to lift the level and quality of insurance broking.

As with everything in life, the cheapest is not necessarily the best. When arranging insurance it's easy to take short cuts and look for the cheapest policy, without considering policy wordings, insurance companies' financial stability, and their claims paying history. Often a wider policy wording does not cost much extra.

In some states, a lender could require you to take out building and contents insurance BEFORE settlement, because you are legally responsible for the property from contract execution, even though technically you don't own it (go figure – real estate law!).

As part of the risk mitigation process it is imperative that as you increase debt, you minimise risk by taking out insurance for the property, principally building and contents (for carpets, light fittings, etc.) and landlords' insurance. In addition it is important to ensure you have adequate personal insurances in place including but not limited to income protection, life insurance and trauma cover.

It is also VERY important that you insure to the correct amount, otherwise underinsurance can cause substantial problems.

Rest assured, you don't want to be one of those families on the nightly news whose house burns down and there is no insurance, or one parent becomes ill and can't work, then can't afford treatment and they have to sell their house to pay the bills. These scenarios happen every day – please don't add to the statistics!

Case Study – *Jason*

Jason bought an investment property and insured the building and contents for $200,000 to save some money on the annual premium. The property was worth $300,000.

His house was located in a high fire risk area and burnt down on a total fire ban day.

When he went to claim his insurance, as he only insured it for $200,000 and not the $300,000 it was worth (i.e. 66% of its value), the insurance company were entitled to only pay him 66% of the amount insured, because the property was underinsured (ask your insurance broker to explain the implications of underinsurance to you. Underinsuring is effectively 'co insurance', as you are effectively agreeing to take on a percentage of the total insurance risk). He received $132,000 benefit, payment leaving him $138,000 short when rebuilding the property. Ouch!

Landlord's insurance can cover you for a number of events including:
- Malicious Damage to the Property
- Loss of Rent
- Accidental Damage
- Fixtures & Fittings
- Public Liability Insurance

Final Stage

QUANTITY SURVEYOR

To receive your full entitlement of tax benefits as a property investor, it's important to obtain a tax depreciation schedule by engaging a quantity surveying firm.

Quantity surveyors have usually completed an appropriate tertiary degree course and undertaken work experience which qualifies them for membership of the Australian Institute of Quantity Surveyors.

As advisors they estimate and monitor construction costs, from the feasibility stage of a project through to the completion of the construction period. When construction is complete the quantity surveyor can produce depreciation schedules of the various project components and advise on realistic insurance replacement costs.

You provide this report to your accountant each year when they lodge your tax return.

Just like when baking a cake, you need to combine all of the ingredients, using the correct method and in the correct order, to get the best possible result. Leave out ingredients and your cake will fall flat!

The same applies to property investing, and the investors that I have seen make the biggest mistakes are those who left out some of the experts along the way, engaged them in the wrong order or at the wrong time.

KEY POINTS

- Remember, this is a property business you are establishing (or running). Always engage professionals as part of the buying process. They are experts in their field for legitimate reasons, and doing it all alone can often be a false economy.

- As you are in the property investment 'business', treat it as such by keeping appropriate records.

- Take note of which experts to engage and when.

- Missing out on engaging these experts could cost you more money than engaging their services – consider risk reduction, time saving and the fact that you aren't an expert yourself as reasons to engage experts.

Bonus Materials
Visit www.propertymavens.com.au to download our free Landlord Record Keeping book and other free buyer resources.

NOTES

STEP

Research, Select and Assess

5

Now that you've improved your money mindset, you understand your personal risk, you have developed your strategy and you've engaged your team of experts, the next step is to decide what to buy, where to buy and to start researching and assessing opportunities.

While some opportunities may look good on the surface, without doing your due diligence you could be saddled with a property that doesn't perform as it should, costing you money in the long-term. Regardless of what the salesman says (whether they are a sales agent, project marketer, property spruiker, developer or 'expert'), BUYER BEWARE is always the rule of thumb to work with when purchasing property.

By understanding the various property types available, you'll have a better foundation from which to assess your property investment options.

Property Types

The main residential investment options include buying established property, buying land to stockpile and/or build on or buying property off the plan.

The following information outlines the risks and benefits associated with investing in these types of property.

Buying Established Property

The argument for buying established property is that when you buy a property which is over 10 years old you aren't paying a developer a profit (as they already made their profit in the original sale). Also, as the building has already depreciated, you are buying it for a higher percentage of land value and lower percentage of building value overall. At a minimum you want to aim to invest for 50% land value (land to asset (building) ratio).

When creating wealth, land increases in value while buildings depreciate, hence the depreciation tax allowance and deferred tax benefit for buildings as they age.

How do we determine land value? Logic would argue that the bigger the land size, the greater the growth. However, this isn't always the case, as you can see in the following chart.

House A is a 10-year-old, two storey 2 bedroom townhouse in an inner-city suburb just 3km from Melbourne's CBD. This property is on **85m2** of land and is valued at $800,000.

House B is a 10-year-old, single storey 3 bedroom house in the suburbs 35km from Melbourne's CBD. The property is on **400m2** of land and is valued at $400,000.

In the chart below we can see that the land value as a percentage of purchase price is much higher for House A than House B, even though House A is on a much smaller block of land.

LAND VALUE AS A PERCENTAGE OF PURCHASE PRICE

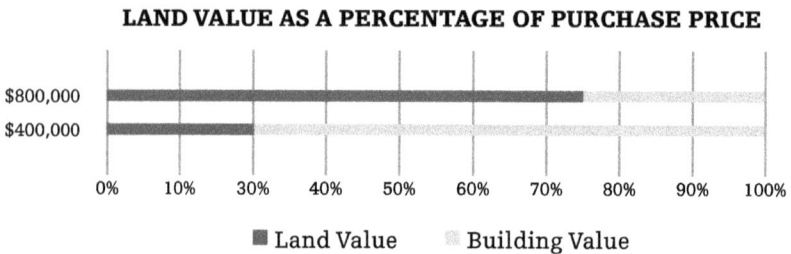

Land Value ■   Building Value

While House A is located just 3km from the CBD, House B is in an outer suburban area where the house and land is much larger. However, there is plenty of ongoing supply due to the area being a 'growth corridor'. The location, lack of infrastructure and supply factors keep price growth flatter and the value of the land per square metre is lower to begin with. This means the majority of the purchase price is tied up in the building.

As you can see, supply and demand are the factors that truly contribute to land value, rather than size. Because the demand for inner-city property is so much higher, the land value of those properties is also much higher than the land value of 'like' properties in the outer suburbs. Note this isn't about the ratio of building to land (i.e. the land size versus the building size) but about the ratio of the **value of the land as a % of the purchase price.**

Apartment blocks are another clear example of land value versus building value. If you buy one apartment in a group of 10, then you own a 1/10th share of the land, as part of your title to the property. If, however, you buy an apartment in a group of 200, then you only own a 1/200th share of the land as part of your title to the property. There is a massive difference between the two, and therefore a much lower opportunity for the 1/200th land share apartment to increase in value over time compared to the smaller apartment block.

Some benefits of buying established property include but aren't limited to:

- Buying for land to asset ratio, which, on older property, is much higher than for new and off the plan property;

- The capacity to see the finished product when buying it, rather than trying to visualise the finished property, based on drawings alone or a display property;

- The ability to experience spatial awareness, which you can't when buying off the plan;

- The ability to add value to it via manufacturing growth – through development or cosmetic or structural renovation; and

- The ability to settle quickly and derive an income from the property while you are planning to renovate or develop it over time.

The main risk considerations for established properties are selecting the **wrong type of property, buying in the wrong location, not knowing your market (tenant or future buyer), rental yield risk and not understanding the drivers of growth** that make the property a viable purchase.

The most common examples of the property types promoted by wholesalers/project marketers/referrers are off the plan apartments, townhouses and land or house/ land packages, as these are a powerful means of selling residential property.

Off The Plan (OTP)

Off the plan properties refer to house and land, houses, townhouses, and unit and apartment developments where you purchase the property based on the plan of what it will look like upon completion. It will involve a contract of sale pertaining to ownership of a specific land or unit lot, and will contain a substantial number of clauses, usually in favour of the developer. Often there are 'sunset' clauses which allow the developer to withdraw from the executed contract of sale after a specified period of time without penalty, sometimes for no reason at all.

Strategies promoted to sell such property include buy, hold and reside; buy, hold and rent; and buy and flip for profit (trading).

Flipping is speculative as it is based upon the premise of buying a property at today's value, while receiving the benefit of reduced stamp duty concessions. It assumes market forces will continue to drive increases in demand up over supply, and that the investor will therefore obtain a capital gain by the time settlement arrives (from 6 – 36 months away). If you have good market timing, then money can be made. However, this is frequently by good luck rather than by genuine research and due diligence. Conversely, if you get the timing wrong, you could potentially lose money by the time settlement arrives, which has been evidenced in the past. It's not uncommon to see a completed new apartment for resale for less money than what it cost the initial buyer to purchase it.

Case study: *Julie and Kenneth*

Julie and Kenneth were in their early 50s and decided they need to plan for retirement as their superannuation fund balances were inadequate.

Like many others, they didn't seek professional advice regarding planning, investing or structuring from a qualified property adviser/buyer agent, accountant or financial planner. They also didn't realise they were low risk profile investors.

They read some articles, attended a property seminar and decided on buying an apartment. They started looking in bayside Melbourne, specifically near St Kilda.

In 2009 they bought a one-bedroom apartment (off the plan) in a smallish group of 35 apartments in St Kilda East, after being told that St Kilda East was the next best place to buy for those who could not afford St Kilda. It would benefit from 'ripple effect' capital growth. They paid $410,000, borrowing 100% plus costs, using their home as security for the property.

They settled the property in 2010 and leased it out.

In late 2013, an analysis identified that the high rental property supply, low income, above average unemployment levels and potential for future oversupply of property combined with low migration to the suburb would all contribute to retarding the opportunity for capital growth in the suburb. Based on these factors, this property showed little opportunity to outperform the average from a capital growth perspective over the longer term.

At that point, I appraised their property at $390,000, indicating a potential loss of $20,000 plus costs if they sold. Unable to reconcile the bad news, Julie and Kenneth elected to hold onto the property, effectively burying their heads in the sand.

In late 2015 Julie and Kenneth decided to sell the property. Their rent had been declining steadily each year due to the increasing supply of hundreds of new apartments being built in the area. This time the property was appraised at $360,000 to $370,000.

The auction campaign failed; however, the property did sell three weeks later for $355,000, resulting in a $55,000 equity loss plus costs, of which they had borrowed 100%. The debt now needs to be repaid.

Considering the lost time (six years) and the opportunity cost had they invested successfully instead, the result is an estimated loss overall of over $100,000 plus.

Risk Rating: 7 - 8/10 moderate risk profile, but higher if intending to flip or trade on or before settlement.

Note – Risk levels are individual. For the purposes of providing a benchmark, I will rate each property type/ strategy out of 10 from the perspective of an investor with a 'prudent/moderate' risk profile. This is subjective, however, and your opinion may differ based on your own risk personal profile.

Some benefits of investing in off the plan properties are:

- The ability to purchase the property in advance of commencement of construction means there can be stamp duty savings, with savings in some states being much more significant than others as they vary from state to state;

- It also gives the buyer additional time to continue to save for costs and/or a bigger deposit, while having secured the property at today's price;

- Some states offer first home owner grants that only apply to new or off the plan property purchases but not established property purchases; and

- It allows foreign investors to purchase property in Australia where they are otherwise restricted from buying in the established marketplace.

The main risk considerations for off the plan properties are **market value risk, construction risk, settlement risk, rental yield risk, developer risk and builder risk** (refer to Appendix 3 – Common Property Investment and Development Risks for more information).

Developing
Developing is when you change the nature of the land by constructing property for profit. It could be a simple subdivision of a block, developing a single unit at the back of an existing house, developing a few units or townhouses on an empty block, or building a low rise residential apartment complex. Developing can have potentially high returns, which is why it appeals to so many investors, but these returns reflect the fact that this is a high-risk strategy.

Developing is a business and should be treated as such, given there can be a lot of money at stake, and there are many opportunities for issues to arise.

As a rule of thumb, when assessing an opportunity, costs should be allowed for on the basis of approximately one third being the Gross Realisable Value (GRV), which includes one third for the cost of the land and Development

Application (DA), approximately one third for construction costs, and approximately one third allocated to profit.

Banks will usually only lend 65% of the GRV and may need a percentage of sales to be committed off the plan before distributing funds for commencement. By only providing 65% the developer has to have some 'skin' in the game via equity contributions and profit being at risk.

Risk Rating: 9-10/10 moderate risk profile

The main risk considerations for developing are **acquisition risk, overcapitalising, marketing risk, finance risk, settlement risk and builder risk** (refer to Appendix 3 – Common Property Investment and Development Risks for more information).

The risks can be quite extensive and I am only touching the surface with some of the risks identified above. Substantial and further education and research regarding developing is required before you proceed down this path as it is very, very easy to get wrong!

HOW TO MINIMISE YOUR RISK
Know your strategy before purchasing the property
You should know your timeframes, tax structuring, suburb research, target market for resale, budget, borrowing capacity, required minimum block sizes, researched local

council and town planning requirements/restrictions, site topography and orientation, significant trees or obstacles, neighbourhood character, utilities and have interviewed and decided who will do the building work and at what price and importantly, what your end goal is BEFORE you even look at any property to purchase.

Do your feasibility study before purchasing the property
It is imperative that you do a feasibility study of the property BEFORE you submit any offers. Ideally you will have an idea of timing, taxation issues, building, finance and other costs. If the numbers stack up but you have to wait for the market demand to increase until it is viable to develop, then you may choose to proceed. If the numbers don't stack up – walk away. There is no point trying to convince yourself that you can take shortcuts to compensate because this will lead to mistakes, not meeting the market's demands and ultimately a loss. Find a property where the numbers do stack up so you can make an offer and stick to your limit.

Know your market
You need to do your research and understand who the end buyer of your developed property is, before you purchase and spend money. This enables you to design to their requirements, therefore increasing your chances of selling the property for a profit once you have met the market's demands.

Don't overcapitalise

Developers and their architects can get excited using materials that appeal to them personally and then end up running over budget, or they think their market is more high-end that it actually needs to be. In short, they lose sight of their development being a business and they make it personal. The same issue can occur in renovations, when renovators get excited and start running over budget because they want to do an exceptional job.

In both scenarios they may try to recoup the additional costs by adding them to the sale price. This can price them out of the market because higher prices may force buyers into a better suburb or to a property with a perceived better value.

Note – the ability for an architectural firm and renovator to manage the budget for design and fit out is paramount! You need to make sure you engage professionals who have a track record of not just being good at design, but of being accountable and excellent at managing their budgets!

Case Study – *Andrea and Greg*

Andrea and Greg liked the idea of developing so they bought a property with the intention of subdividing the block, building on the back and renovating the front house. They weren't quite sure which they would live in and if they would keep one and sell the other, or keep both and rent one.

Against advice, they didn't speak to an accountant so had no idea of the tax and GST implications for the strategies they were considering, and they weren't even sure who's name (or which entity) they should have bought it in.

They bought a four bedroom home unconditionally at auction, only knowing the estimated size of the land required for subdivision in the local area. By not speaking to their accountant first and knowing who the purchaser should be, they neglected to put the correct name on the contract of sale and would be subject to double stamp duty if they needed to change ownership for tax reasons (as part of the development strategy).

They also neglected to seek finance advice on development funding, so didn't know whether they would even qualify for the finance to develop, or what timeframe might apply to the provision of development funds.

After buying unconditionally at auction, Andrea went to the local council to learn more about getting a development application approved.

To her horror, Andrea found out that to develop what, how and where they wanted to, they would need to REMOVE the fourth bedroom of the house, which needed to be knocked down to make way for parking! This now turned an appealing 4 bedroom house into a less appealing three bedroom house.

This research should have been obtained before they bid at auction and this is just the beginning of what could continue to be a very tough lesson for them (refer Step 4 Engage Your Team of Experts).

Land Banking

Land banking is often included as part of the development process. This is the process of securing future property development sites at today's price and stock piling them (often through using an option contract). Many large developers buy farms, tracts of land and greenfield sites to ensure they have ongoing opportunities for future developments. Over time they rezone the land, put in infrastructure, subdivide the land into smaller lots and on sell them.

On a smaller scale, small developers also buy land in inner and mid-ring suburbs of cities and develop them over time, often quite successfully. This is generally because land is in low supply but increasing demand allows development of the site into denser multi-unit developments such as townhouses or even small low rise apartment buildings.

Risk Rating: 8 - 9/10 moderate risk profile

The benefits of land banking are:

- The ability to secure land for development before it is required;

- The ability to secure land in flatter markets at more affordable rates; and

- The ability to plan developments into the future because land has been already secured.

The main risk considerations for land baking are **market value risk and cash flow** (refer to Appendix 3 – Common Property Investment and Development Risks for more information).

Note - Refer to the case study on page 12 & 13

Renovation and Adding Value

Renovating is simply improving an existing property to sell or lease at a higher value than the investor would have received originally. This could be a cosmetic or structural renovation to a tired or out-dated property, or demolishing and rebuilding.

Risk Rating: 6 - 8/10 moderate risk profile

Some benefits of renovating and adding value are:

- The ability to manufacture immediate capital growth through cosmetic or structural renovation;

- The ability to leverage more debt as a result of manufacturing capital growth to buy more property; and

- The ability to increase rental return (yield) by improving the property.

The main risk considerations for renovating and adding value are **overcapitalisation, market value risk, rental yield risk and settlement risk** (refer to Appendix 3 – Common Property Investment and Development Risks for more information).

10 in 10

This is a blanket strategy that is promoted as a means of building a large portfolio quickly, and is based on you buying 10 properties in 10 years (or similar). Generally this strategy is based on buying low value property that is neutrally or positively cash flowed, and relies on increases in capital growth and yield to continue to leverage into other properties. It could also entail investing in areas that are higher risk and higher return such as mining towns.

Risk Rating: 7-9/10 moderate risk profile

Some benefits of following a 10 in 10 strategy are:

- At a minimum it is a strategy to work towards, even if not tailored personally; and

- It can be argued that getting into the market and realising small gains is better than not being in the market at all.

The main risk considerations that a one size fits all approach (such as a 10 in 10 strategy) may not take into consideration are **risk profile, attitude and appetite**. Investors should also understand that achieving property prosperity isn't about having a large portfolio with dozens or hundreds of properties, but about having the right number to achieve the end goal you have in mind, while managing your personal cash flow considerations and allowing you to have a degree of lifestyle in the process. Remember, the more property you have, the more expensive and time-consuming it is to manage. There can also be substantial maintenance or vacancy issues over time if you don't buy well, and you may even need to manage the property managers that you have engaged to work on your behalf.

Lease Options

Lease options are a short-term strategy where you have the option to purchase a property, lease it immediately and hold, or renovate to add value. The contract itself is made up of a standard tenancy agreement with renovation rights as an option contract.

An option contract is an agreement for the right to purchase a property, but not the obligation to purchase. It includes three features:

1 The option fee is established. This is the amount the purchaser agrees to pay for the option to purchase the property and is non-refundable in the event that the contract isn't executed. Fees can vary according to the property, the supply and demand factors in the market at the time and the possible usage opportunities of the property/site.

2 It establishes the sale price of the contract to be paid at the date the option is executed.

3 It establishes the length of time/date the option is available for before it expires.

Risk Rating: 6 - 9 /10 for a moderate risk profile

The benefit of a lease option is that it provides flexibility while leaving your options open. Having secured the right but not the obligation to buy the property at an agreed point in time for a small fee enables you to gain from potential upswing in the property's value (in an increasing market); while if the market decreases in that time, you can forgo the option fee and walk away.

The main risk consideration for lease options is **renovating.**

The lease portion of the contract may be inflated with any amount over the market rental going towards the build-up of a deposit.

If renovating whilst leasing and having access to the property, the opportunity to add value may increase the value of the property before settlement and therefore may allow the purchaser to create or grow a deposit in the form of equity, and therefore enable them to borrow 100% of the balance to finance the purchase.

If the purchaser doesn't qualify for finance, the risk is they can't settle and lose/can't recoup the renovation costs they have injected into the property. In addition, and depending on the contract conditions, the purchaser may be required to settle.

House and Land Packages
This is where you can buy a property based on the concept/plan of the property being sold attached to a parcel or specific lot of land. There are usually two contracts provided – one is the building contract and the other is the land contract of sale. These could be to the same or different parties.

Risk Rating: 7/10 for a moderate risk profile

The benefits of investing in house and land packages are:

• The ability to purchase the property in advance of commencement of construction means there can be stamp duty savings, with savings in some states being much more significant than others as they vary from state to state;

• It also gives the buyer additional time to continue to save for costs and a bigger deposit while having secured the property at today's price; and

- Some state offer first home owner grants that only apply to new or off the plan property but not established property.

The main risk considerations for house and land packages are similar to off the plan properties – **market value risk, construction risk, settlement risk, rental yield risk, developer risk and builder risk** (refer to Appendix 3 – Common Property Investment and Development Risks for more information).

NRAS - National Rental Affordability Scheme

NRAS is a Federal Government initiative that was introduced in July 2008 as part of the Federal Government's GFC building industry stimulus package. It was designed to give the building industry a boost and address the growing shortfall of affordable accommodation. It is a not a property investment scheme.

The initiative was designed to drive more affordable housing to be built in areas of high rental demand for tenants within capped household income levels. These tenants may include, singles, sole parents and families. The scheme provides a 20% discounted rental return based on market value, while providing investors with a Commonwealth financial incentive of $7486 per annum plus a State/Territory incentive (this varies from state to state and is indexed to inflation for a 10 year period) to support the initiative. In

Victoria the state incentive is $2495, providing a combined total of $9981 per annum for the financial year ending 2013.

These incentives only apply to brand new property that must not have been previously tenanted, which is why property spruikers have attached it to off the plan properties. NRAS provides affordable housing options to the community, which is distinctly different to social housing, however, tenants' or buyers' perceptions may make this difficult to rent or resell down the track.

This initiative expired in 2014, due to the Federal Government not extending it.

Risk Rating: 7 - 8/10 for a moderate risk profile

Some benefits of taking advantage of the NRAS are

- For some buyers it will enable them to better cash flow their investment; and

- The additional funds can be used to pay down debt and generate neutral to positive cash flow more quickly.

The main risk considerations for this investment strategy are as per off the plan properties – **market value risk, construction risk, settlement risk, rental yield risk, developer risk and builder risk** (refer to Appendix 3 –

Common Property Investment and Development Risks for more information).

However, this strategy carries with it the following additional risks:

UNDERLYING ASSET

While receiving an annual incentive of approximately $10,000 per annum is attractive, this is a benefit of investing and, like depreciation benefits, it shouldn't be the driver or main reason to purchase a property. It should only be treated as a bonus. The property still requires the foundation of a good investment (all the usual drivers need to be present) from a capital growth or rental income perspective and from an exit strategy perspective. The main reason to consider investing with this type of incentive is as a means of holding onto the property and funding it for long enough to enable capital growth over time, but that assumes it will grow in value over time and the only way to determine that is to do your due diligence.

If it's the type of property that isn't likely to grow as a result of growth drivers that are missing or an oversupply in the market and therefore lack of demand when exiting, then it may not stack up as a good investment option.

PROPERTY MANAGEMENT AND HEAD LEASE ISSUES

Unlike a standard rental property, there are a number of restrictions as to who the tenant can be in terms of their income levels. Therefore the market for tenants is smaller than a standard rental property and this increases the risk to investors. This is, however, offset by the anticipated demand of tenants wanting discounted rental accommodation to be high.

NRAS requires that tenancy management services comply with the residential tenancy legislation and relevant tenancy and property management regulations in the State or Territory in which the dwelling is located. Investors should note that failure by a tenancy manager to comply with the requirements of the Scheme may impact on your right to receive the National Rental Incentive, and may result in an allocation being revoked if the conditions of your allocation are not complied with. Who you engage as 'specialist NRAS' property manager will be extremely important, as they should provide a level of service that protects your incentive

In addition, and depending on which company has the head lease arrangement, you will be asked to sign a lease agreement that may not give you choice or flexibility to nominate or select your own property manager. This is highly risky in that if for any reason you are not satisfied with the level of service they provide as property manager, you do not have the ability to sack them and engage another firm. There is therefore a lower requirement to deliver exceptional service because they effectively have you legally bound to using their services. Do you really want to bind your hands like that?

If not, delete contract clauses that restrict you in this manner before signing or request to buy the property with a different NRAS provider, as some developers can assist with this option. If the selling agent or developer can't offer that, then find a different agent who can.

Self-Managed Super Funds (SMSFs)
SMSFs are a tax-concessioned vehicle through which you can invest to build your retirement nest egg. However, an SMSF is, as the name suggests, self-managed.

SMSFs shouldn't be seen as a 'strategy' for investing, UNLESS it's presented this way by your accountant or financial planner, as part of your overall financial or tax plan.

In other words, there are substantial benefits to investors when using this type of structure to invest, however you should ONLY consider purchasing property within a SMSF when the recommendation is advice driven by your advisor and NOT by project marketers or spruikers, who are recommending this as a wealth creation strategy so they can sell property. If you come across one of these 'wealth creation' companies who are promoting SMSFs as an investment 'strategy', I recommend you do not take any action unless you have first spoken to your expert advisor, as they are aware of your complete financial circumstances and will advise you accordingly if this structure is appropriate and if you have sufficient funds to warrant the cost of setting one up and paying for the ongoing annual compliance fees.

There are many restrictions when buying property within SMSFs that don't apply outside of these structures, and trustees have substantial obligations in ensuring they are meeting all of their compliance requirements and the SMSF's investment strategy when purchasing property within their fund.

It is also costly to establish a SMSF and there are annual compliance costs which can also be very expensive, so it simply isn't for everyone. At a minimum you would need at least $150,000 in your superannuation fund for it to be financially viable, and even then it may not be a good option for you.

Some restrictions include but aren't limited to:

• Reduced borrowing capacity (lower loan to value ratios)

• Higher interest rates on loans

- No ability to withdraw equity from the asset to leverage into other property

- No ability to develop property within a SMSF whilst you still have the borrowings in place

- Expensive set up and ongoing compliance/auditing costs

- Additional time commitment from trustees to ensure compliance

There are many accountants and financial planners, when recommending the implementation of a SMSF, also recommend the engagement of a buyer agent's service because mistakes such as buying the wrong type of property or completing a contract incorrectly could make your SMSF non-compliant. This can lead to many ensuing problems such as having the ATO audit your fund and penalise you for non-compliance or even forcing you to sell the asset, possibly costing you hundreds of thousands. Other mistakes, such as having the wrong titles, can also be costly and could result in you having to set up additonal bare trusts at substantial ongoing accouting and compliance costs to your Fund.

Many investors buy property off the plan, NRAS or house and land packages to put into their SMSFs so all of the same risks considerations that apply to those strategies apply when buying them in an SMSF. More importantly ask yourself, is the property likely to perform based on the growth drivers you have researched? Does it have the right level of land value percentage you need to create wealth? If not, seek to buy something within your SMSF that will.

Risk Rating: 8-9/10 for a moderate risk profile due to the increased complexity regarding this structure

Where to Buy – Drivers of Growth

Establishing a prosperous, sustainable property portfolio isn't just about your capacity to hold it over time, but is also about the opportunities for sustainable growth over time. Understanding the drivers of growth, and whether they are temporary and unsustainable or permanent and sustainable, will enable you to be more selective with your investments.

Macro and microeconomic drivers influence growth.

Macroeconomics is the study of the current Australian economic market conditions and where they sit in relation to the rest of the world. Broadly in relation the property market, these encompass supply and demand, which are driven by:

- Population growth
- Land availability
- Housing starts
- Mineral explorations
- Tourism
- Infrastructure investment (state and federal) and business investment in infrastructure

Microeconomics relate to events in regional areas and are often used when 'hot spotting' areas for sustainable future capital growth or rental increases.

Broadly in relation to increases in the property market, these encompass:

- Population growth and population migration (through the provision of sustainable employment opportunities, especially where salaries are strong so disposable income is often higher)

- Amenities such as the provision of schools and hospitals to support a growing population

- Decreases in the property market can be as a result of:
  ° Over-supply of property
  ° Primary industry closing down (e.g. a car manufacturing plant as a primary employer may shut down)

By researching both macro and microeconomic drivers, an investor can gain a better understanding of the likely level of risk attached to property they are considering buying in a particular region or city, from an entry, hold and exit perspective. Refer to Appendix 2 at the back for useful resources.

FACTORS DRIVING RENTAL RETURN

If you purchase property in areas where there is high demand but limited supply, especially for a particular demographic, such as students sharing, professionals or families, or if it is in a location that is in high demand but limited supply, then your opportunities for regular rental increases and long terms tenancies improve.

If it's the type of property that is unique, has wow factor or appeals to prospective home owners, then your chances of renting to those who want that lifestyle or property type will be in demand.

Basic property features that will increase your chances of leasing the property easily include efficient heating and cooling, good airflow and light, a quiet neighborhood, low maintenance gardens and privacy.

You can also add value by appealing to the corporate rental market, which is a way of obtaining a higher yield year in and year out.

KEY POINTS

- Buy for land value as a percentage (land to asset ratio) and not for land size or building to land ratio.

- Make sure you fully understand the risks associated with the different types of property before you buy anything.

- Match your risk profile to the appropriate risk type, so you can sleep at night while implementing your investment strategy.

- Remember, depreciation, negative gearing and NRAS rebates are a benefit of investing and should NEVER be a driver or strategy to invest.

- Use investment structures like SMSFs or Trusts when it is advice driven by your expert advisor and NOT when property driven by property spruikers/project marketers/wholesalers/research houses/clubs, etc. as their advice isn't independent.

- Understand the drivers of growth, research and invest accordingly.

- Know who your prospective tenant is when you buy.

NOTES

STEP 6

Negotiate the Offer

Real estate is a bit of a 'game', so either learn the rules or engage someone who understands them (See Step 4 Engage Your Team of Experts). Additionally, the rules of the game differ from state to state due to varying legislation, so don't make the mistake of thinking that each state's rules are the same.

There are rules that selling agents (players on the selling team) need to abide by, there are rules buyers and buyers agents need to abide by (players on the buying team), and there is an 'umpire' in every state, otherwise known as Consumer Affairs.

Each state has a Real Estate Institute body that operates as the 'players association', or the peak professional association for both members and the general public. In some states players may voluntarily join the association (as in Victoria), whereas in others membership is mandatory (like Western Australia).

In Victoria for example, the Real Estate Institute of Victoria (renamed REIV July 1, 1985) operates in this capacity. Its members specialise in all facets of real estate, including: residential sales, commercial and industrial sales, auctions, business broking, buyers' agency/advocacy, property management, owners' corporations' management and valuations.

The Rules

The following rules apply specifically to Victoria, but the premise follows for other states. Please refer to the Appendix for your local 'umpire' details or see the BONUS section at the end of this chapter for more information.

Real estate pricing and advertising[1]
Property advertising must not be misleading or deceptive. It is illegal for a seller or agent to misrepresent a property in any way when advertising or marketing that property, whether verbally or in writing and photographs.

It is illegal for an agent to advertise or advise (whether orally or in writing) a prospective buyer of a price that is less than the seller's auction reserve price or asking price, or if there is no such price , the agent's current estimate of the likely selling price.

This is known as underquoting.

An agent must:
- Give an accurate appraisal of the market price of the property, and
- Update the advertised price if it changes during the sales campaign.

---

1 Consumer Affairs Victoria - *Real Estate - a guide for buyers and sellers*

A seller's reserve, or asking price, is the lowest price a seller is prepared to accept for their property. It's called the reserve price for an auction and the asking price for a private sale.

The seller's reserve price is usually set on the day of the auction. It may be higher than the advertised price if the seller believes several genuine buyers are interested in the property.

If a seller advises an agent of their asking or reserve price during the marketing campaign, then the agent cannot advertise the property below that price.

An agent's estimated selling price is the price the agent estimates a property is likely to attract, based on their experience and knowledge of the market. In Victoria, if recorded as a range, the top of the estimated selling price range must not be more than 10 per cent of the bottom figure. For example, a quoted range of $400,000 to $440,000 is $400,000 plus 10 per cent.

The agent's estimated selling price does not have to be the same as the seller's asking or reserve price. If a seller has not provided an agent with an asking or reserve price, the property must not be advertised for sale at a price that is less than the agent's estimated selling price.

Underquoting[2]

Underquoting is when an agent misleads a prospective buyer about the likely selling price of a property for sale. Examples of underquoting are when a property is advertised or quoted to a prospective buyer at a price that is less than:

- The seller's asking price or auction reserve price
- The agent's estimate of the selling price
- A genuine offer or expression of interest by a prospective buyer that the vendor has refused

Comparing the initial advertised price with the sale price is not evidence of underquoting.

BE AWARE OF UNDERQUOTING

Doing your homework before you buy will help you to understand the market and be a better judge of property sale prices.

- Research the market value of property in your preferred areas by searching the internet, attending auctions, speaking with a variety of estate agents and monitoring auction results.

---

2 Consumer Affairs Victoria - *Real Estate Guidelines for real estate salespeople – price advertising and underquoting*

- Use the agent's estimated selling price as a guide only. The agent represents the seller but must be fair and honest with buyers.

- Ask the agent to justify their advertised price by providing recent comparable sales evidence. They should have knowledge of the market in the area to support their estimate.

- The seller is unlikely to set their auction reserve price until the day of the auction (and isn't obliged to do so any earlier). The reserve price decided on the day might be above the advertised price.

- Do not allow emotion to cloud your judgment and be realistic about the likely selling price

Note – If you have evidence that an agent has underquoted the selling price, contact Consumer Affairs in your state. If you want a more immediate response to the issue, however, you can contact Consumer Affairs for information to clarify the matter, and then also contact the agent or their Principal directly (now being fully informed) to inform them that you are going to lodge a formal complaint with Consumer Affairs. Often this is sufficient to get the agent to adjust the pricing accordingly per their legal obligations (if they have in fact been underquoting).

Sometimes the reality is that it's a dirty game being played, but that's why the umpire exists. Often the lack of transparency by some agents, such as not declaring a price in writing, contributes to the problem. Although legally there is no requirement for them to disclose a price in writing in some states, morally one could argue otherwise. If this lack of transparency frustrates you, support agents who are transparent, don't deal with those who aren't, and formally alert your umpire to genuine issues in writing.

Knowledge is power, so be informed! When unethical agents know they are dealing with savvy and informed buyers, they are less likely to try and get away with unethical and ILLEGAL practices, especially if they know you will hold them to account.

Note:
NSW – New underquoting laws apply to the sale of NSW residential property from 1 January 2016. The underquoting reforms are designed to stop real estate agents understating property prices.

QLD – Legislation banning real estate agents from providing price guides has been passed by the Queensland parliament. In short, prices are no longer allowed to be advertised at all for properties being auctioned. It is up to the consumer to effectively guess what the price is likely to be. Go figure!

BONUS – Visit www.propertymavens.com.au to obtain buying, selling and price quoting guidelines for real estate in each state. These resources will be extremely important when negotiating to buy property, whether by private sale or auction.

Negotiating an Offer

When buying property, you will purchase either by private sale (treaty), at auction or post auction. However, the success or failure of establishing your portfolio is more than simply purchasing a property, and often comes down to your ability or inability to successfully negotiate a result in your favour.

The following are the most common methods of sale of property and comments are based on the assumption that you have done your due diligence, have a strong understanding of the market value of the property, have assessed your cash flow and have a fixed budget when negotiating or bidding at auction.

Remember to:

- Make sure you have the contract reviewed BEFORE you place an offer on the property, and

- Include a clause for building and pest inspections (worded in your favour as the buyer) or attend to these BEFORE the auction (refer Step 4 Engage Your Team of Experts).

Case Study – *Bruce*

Remember Miranda in Step 4? After she settled on her property and moved in, we met her neighbour who bought the matching townhouse 12 months prior to Miranda.

Bruce is a Licensed Property Valuer and he wisely recognised the property to be an investment grade asset as well as a suitable home for himself and his partner, Storm. He attended the auction and bought the property three days after it was passed in at auction. He failed, however, to include a clause requiring a building and pest inspection as he didn't do one prior to attending the auction (Bruce has a high risk profile).

As his property was built by the same developer at the same time as Miranda's, it had similar issues to the ones revealed in Miranda's building inspection report. Needless to say, he wasn't very happy to hear about the $35,000 of repairs that Miranda was implementing, given the very strong likelihood that he would have to attend to these one day himself, but out of his own pocket and not the vendor's!

Always, always do a building and pest inspection – even if you are a professional who in one form or another works in the property sector or you have a high risk profile. There's no point winning financially at one end and then giving the win away by not doing all of your due diligence.

Remember, in all situations described below you will be up against seasoned professionals and highly experienced negotiators. If negotiating isn't one of your strong points, then ensure you are protected during this process by engaging a professional who understands real estate law, or bring someone along who is also highly experienced in this area.

Important – if you have a friend or family member bidding on your behalf at auction, make sure you have formally engaged them to bid for you, because technically when the hammer goes down on THEIR bid, THEY have bought the property and are putting themselves at risk by doing so. There are documented occasions where someone has 'bid' on behalf of a friend who has panicked and left them with the purchase. When buying at auction you are dealing under Real Estate Law, so don't enter this situation naively – especially if you are the friend or family member doing the bidding!

Buying by private sale (private treaty)
This is when a property is placed on the market and advertised for sale with a price declared in the form of a single price, price range or frustratingly, not at all!

Buyers deal directly with the real estate agent and make offers to and negotiate via the agent.

Remember, everything is negotiable. Whether it is the length of the settlement period, the size of the deposit, time required to allow for research and inspections such as building and pest, early access to the property for renovations, etc. However, while everything is negotiable, both parties in the transaction need to agree to the terms.

At this point there may be a number of outcomes. Hopefully you will reach an agreement that satisfies you both. Remain civil throughout the process and be realistic about pricing. Often it's about securing an asset at fair market value that will perform above the average, as opposed to driving a hard bargain at the risk of missing out altogether.

Outcome 1 – No agreement is achieved

1 Your offer is rejected without a counter offer and you don't wish to change your terms or price.

2 Your offer is rejected without a counter offer and you decide to modify your offer by changing the price, the terms or both. The vendor doesn't accept your new offer or counter offer.

3 Your offer is countered and you go back and forth until an agreement can't be reached and a stalemate occurs.

If you reach the third scenario, part ways on friendly terms but stipulate that you will no longer be accountable for your last offer and formalise it by providing written notice of your withdrawal from the negotiations.

Outcome 2 – Agreement is achieved
1   Your offer may be accepted as you have presented.

2   Your offer may be rejected without a counter offer, at which point you either offer more money, amend your terms or both.

3   You go back and forth until an agreement is reached confirming the price, terms and settlement date.

Congratulations! The contract is executed by all parties and you leave the negotiation with your own copy of the executed contract. The next step is to provide a copy to all of your respective experts to ensure the process of settlement gets underway. This is especially important if any terms/ conditions were included such as finance approval and of course you need to ensure you pay the deposit as agreed.

Note – In some states a 'cooling off' period applies after an offer has been accepted and executed, but as these vary from state to state, or don't actually exist at all, you will need to research the state that you are buying in.

Buying at (public) auction

This is where the property is placed on the market for sale by public auction on a particular date and time. Generally a price range is declared, however, sometimes no price is declared at all!

Where possible, avoid buying at auction. However if you can't, consider presenting an offer before the auction. The selling agent is legally obliged to present it to the vendor (unless instructed by the vendor in writing otherwise), and putting the offer in writing makes it legitimate and worthy of consideration. Depending on the level of interest in the property, the vendor may or may not wish to accept, counter offer or even negotiate your offer.

At a minimum before attending the auction and bidding, do your due diligence by having the contract reviewed and obtaining a building and pest report. Providing you are satisfied with the feedback from each expert, it's time to bid.

Be aware that selling agents and auctioneers use very advanced tactics and methods to create hype and are dependent upon buyers who are overly emotional to drive property prices up.

Auction advertising campaigns that use 'bait' or 'stepped' pricing marketing strategies are designed to encourage buyers to attend auctions and drive bidding momentum up to their maximum (but often inadequate) bidding limit, which falsely gives the impression that there is greater demand for a property than there really may be. i.e. those who can't afford the real price but bid anyway, effectively create the heat at the top of their price limit.

As auctions are designed to remove negotiating power from the buyers and to drive buyers into an emotional frenzy, take some of your power back by having other viable properties on the backburner. That way if you miss out on this property, you can pick yourself up, dust yourself off and get on with the next one.

Remember to keep your cash flow figures and budget in mind and stick to that budget. Pay attention to who else is buying. Do they look like a young couple buying their first home, or a family that wants to be in the area for a particular school zone? If so, be aware that they may drive the price up from an emotional perspective, thus creating competition and forcing themselves (or someone else) to pay a price that's above reasonable or market value based on recent sales evidence. In doing so, this actually sets a new market value/level.

Passing in at auction

If your budget permits, you want to be the final bidder so that you have obtained the right to negotiate before the property has been passed in. This is your opportunity to negotiate the best deal you can to secure the property.

1   If you are invited into the property to negotiate, DON'T go inside. Stay outside so you can keep an eye on the other agents and to see if there are other prospective buyers hanging around that they may be talking with. This alleviates the pressure of being inside, being told there are other buyers outside (even when there aren't) and making a negotiation mistake.

It is also necessary for you to obtain some privacy if you need to step away to make a call or confer with a companion regarding the deal.

2   As the highest bidder, you made the last offer so it is now the vendor's turn to move off their reserve in order to commence negotiations. Ask what the reserve is and disclose nothing further until you have an answer from the agent. Once you have it, ask further questions of the agent – can they provide evidence to justify the reserve, where is their comparable sales evidence to support that price?

If the reserve is more than 10% over the quoted price range, and based on the information earlier regarding pricing, ask why the reserve is so high. It may result in the reserve being revised downwards. Remember, you don't have to accept the offer or the terms, as these can be renegotiated also. As an investor you may want to ask for longer settlement or access before settlement to take photos and start showing prospective tenants through the property. Take note however that in some states, auction conditions (i.e. unconditional purchase terms) may continue for a period of time (e.g. 3 days in Victoria) after the publicly advertised auction has failed and the property has passed in.

As when negotiating a private sale, your negotiation could end in a number of outcomes.

Outcome 1 – No agreement is achieved
1 Your offer is rejected without a counter offer and you don't wish to change your terms or price.

2 Your offer is rejected without a counter offer and you decide to modify your offer by changing the price, the terms or both. The vendor doesn't accept your new offer or counter offer.

3 Your offer is countered and you go back and forth until an agreement can't be reached and a stalemate occurs.

If you reach scenario three, as with negotiating a private sale, part ways on friendly terms but stipulate that you will no longer be accountable for your last offer and formalise it by providing written notice of your withdrawal from the negotiations.

Outcome 2 – Agreement is achieved
1 Your offer may be accepted as you have presented.

2 Your offer may be rejected without a counter offer, at which point you either offer more money, amend your terms or both.

3 You go back and forth until an agreement is reached confirming the price, terms and settlement date.

Congratulations! The contract is executed by all parties and you leave the negotiation with your own copy of the executed contract. Just as when buying by private sale, the next step is to provide a copy of the contract to all of your respective experts to ensure the process of settlement gets underway. This is especially important so any terms/conditions that were included (such as finance approval) can be met according to deadlines and of course, you need to ensure you pay the deposit as agreed.

Case Study: *Ryan*

We attended an auction on a client's behalf, acting as his buyer's agent. Having done all our research and due diligence in advance, we were aware of the market value of the property under current market conditions. We also set a clear budget and, if the bidding exceeded this, we were prepared to walk away.

Bidding started at $560,000 and the property was quickly passed in to us on that single bid. The auction marketing campaign had failed, likely because the common practice of price underquoting had resulted in prospective buyers automatically adding too much to the top of the quote range and excluding themselves from participating in the auction.

After the property passed in, negotiations commenced. The vendor's reserve was $620,000. However, after much back and forth the final sale price was $591,000, nearly $30,000 below the vendor's reserve and $30,000 below the property's market value.

The best weapon in negotiation is research

Performing due diligence before making an offer on a property or bidding at auction is the best way investors can ensure they pay a fair market price. It may also give them further negotiating power when they make an offer after the property has passed in at auction.

By having a strong understanding of the market value of property in their preferred areas (which can be researched by searching the internet, attending auctions, speaking with a variety of estate agents and monitoring auction results), investors can:

- determine whether an agent's estimated selling price is realistic;

- ask the agent to justify their advertised price by providing recent comparable sales evidence. They should have knowledge of the market in the area to support their estimate;

- evaluate whether the auction reserve price is a fair representation of the property's market value; and

- make a final decision based on facts rather than emotion.

Case Study: *Research*

What allowed the investor in the previous example to buy a bargain was our research, buying strategy and due diligence.

We had recent comparable sales evidence, so knew the quoted price range was realistic. We knew who we were bidding against, we had our bidding strategy in place, we had vendor and agent intelligence at hand and we knew our clients budget limit.

When the property passed in to us and the reserve was declared, we recognised good value at that price and, using solid negotiation tactics, took full advantage of it. Our client was very much the beneficiary that day!

KEY POINTS

- Learn the rules of the 'game'.

- Know who your local 'umpire' and 'players association' are. They are both there to help you as a consumer.

- Do your research so that you know the market value of the property you want to buy.

- Make sure you have had the contract reviewed BEFORE you place an offer on the property (refer Step 4 Engage Your Team of Experts).

- Remember to include a clause for building and pest inspections or attend to these BEFORE the auction (refer Step 4 Engage Your Team of Experts).

- Get professional help if negotiation isn't your strong point!

NOTES

STEP 7

Review Your Portfolio

Like any asset or investment, you need to keep check on how your property is performing over time. Many investors I come across have no real awareness as to how and at what rate their property has performed, let alone what the opportunity for future growth is like.

If you have invested in managed funds or shares, you will mostly likely receive an Annual Report from the fund manager or company identifying what has transpired during the year from a costs, growth and performance perspective.

Property is no different, however most investors only take into account the costs and tax benefits when they lodge their tax returns, but don't take into account annual growth or ongoing opportunity for growth, from both the perspective of capital and rental growth.

Why and Frequency

The benefit of doing such monitoring is to ensure that your property is still performing to expectation, and that you don't get caught out in the event that the market turns.

Ideally you should revisit the reasons why you bought the property every 12 months to monitor the local situation. However, if the area is in the media or there is unusual activity or talk about the property market there, review more frequently. If you don't stay on top of it, it could cost you dearly!

Example – *Docklands Precinct, Melbourne, Victoria*

Back to the Docklands. When the precinct was approved for development, there was plenty of buzz in the property marketplace. There were opportunities for investors, retailers, small businesses, retirees and home buyers alike to benefit from the development of the precinct, plus the number of jobs that would be created along the way.

Eventually apartment towers went to market for sale and those that saw the vision, had the courage, and bought the sales pitch started to buy into the first few towers, as there was a great opportunity to get in early and ride the growth wave.

Plenty of early buyers benefitted, and then it became quite common to see investors buying up to two or three properties each with the view to 'flip' all or most of them before settlement. This allowed many to make a profit along the way, due to the growth that was being generated by market forces and developers driving price increases every time a new tower was released (often smaller apartments for the same money or more money than earlier towers). There was, however, a downturn in the demand for such property, and eventually an over-supply of stock resulted in prices either dropping or stagnating, and not moving for several years. In addition, many of the 'flippers' got burned as they couldn't off-load their property, which also contributed to prices falling.

Had an early investor kept an eye on what was happening year-on-year in the precinct, other Melbourne CBD developments and the local economy, they could have (and a number did) sold their property early on, taken the profit and reinvested into a new opportunity elsewhere, or simply cashed out altogether.

Many who didn't sell, or bought at the peak of the market upswing, were left with properties whose values stagnated or declined, while demand fizzled and both property and rentals went into oversupply.

Add all of the other apartment precincts around Melbourne that were being developed and settled around the same time, and this contributed to the problem.

It's fair to say it took a number of years before the apartment glut was absorbed from a rental perspective and before there was reasonable price growth.

Don't Fall in Love with Your Property

No matter how new the kitchen is, how beautiful the little courtyard out the back is, or how much space and light is in the entrance, DON'T FALL IN LOVE WITH YOUR PROPERTY!

This is a property **business**, and you need to treat it as such. If you are buying a property to live in, it's ok to be emotional (providing those emotions don't lead you to paying too much for it or buying the wrong property) but it's best to remain detached with investment property.

Getting emotionally involved can make it harder for you to make the right decisions as a **business person**. Falling in love with property makes it harder to cut your losses and sell if it is no longer performing, or unlikely to continue to perform over the longer term. Likewise, staying frozen in fear and distrust can prevent you from achieving your goals altogether.

Understandably if you have been burnt by investing poorly you might prefer to stick your head in the sand, but you are far more likely to get a kick up the backside doing that. These days it is far too easy to get stuck in 'analysis paralysis' and do nothing, get busy and miss the boat or wish you had done something when you had the chance. Sound familiar?

Taking no action is a decision to do nothing, and is often the result of not having adequate **evidence** on which to base a decision OR you are investing beyond your risk profile, attitude or appetite or in property type or strategy that also doesn't match your personal profile, hence the resistance. And, it was probably also the reason why you were burnt in the past.

If you aren't clear on your strategy, haven't confirmed your borrowing capacity and financial situation, have other personal matters clouding your judgment, have too much on your plate, or have been swayed by an article, a friend or an advertisement espousing the next best thing/hotspot/ strategy, then you are letting your emotions guide your investment decisions, rather than acting as a **business owner**.

Often action is required to move past an error and take the steps required to turn the situation into a positive.

Client Case Study – *Justine*

Justine was an experienced investor. She had purchased a property that wasn't performing to expectation and wanted to continue to grow her property portfolio, but this property had performed so poorly that she found herself in a negative equity situation after a period of only having owned the property for three years. Like many investors in this situation, she was uncertain as to what to do with the property moving forward and 'hoped' it would improve but had no evidence to confirm it would.

Had Justine reviewed her portfolio each year she would have been aware of the fact that the main source of local employment in the area had shut down and ceased trading two years earlier. The industry had come to an end and her property's value and opportunity for growth were severely affected, to the point that diligent research indicated there

---

would very little ongoing opportunity for capital or rental growth moving forward. Now fully informed of the likelihood of improvement (or, in this case, the lack of it) Justine was provided with two options – the first being keeping the property, while being fully informed of its opportunity for ongoing capital growth and yield expectations, along with the implications of these.

The second was the option of selling the property. Taking into account the approximate selling costs, reallocation of the loan into a stronger performing property, the entry costs to that property and the time it would take to recoup costs and estimated capital loss as a result of liquidating the poorly performing property, Justine now had factual information on which to base her decision. She could now comfortably take action as a result of being fully informed.

What to Review
MICROECONOMIC INDICATORS
Microeconomic indicators need to be taken into consideration when reviewing your portfolio as well as when determining where to buy in the first place, including:

- What influence are the local factors having?
- What are the levels of employment and economic growth, and are they increasing or decreasing?

- What is the population demographic made up of and is this likely to change?
- What infrastructure is being built by local and state governments?
- What else is driving supply and demand?
- What are the supply levels like for your property type in the suburb vs demand for it ?
- And what else did you take into account when buying in the first instance that you should review?

These need to be researched and analysed, and then you need to make a decision based on the outcome of this research. If you haven't done this before, I encourage you to revisit your property portfolio and start the process to see if you are on track. Start with one property at a time and slowly work your way through them. Expect each property to take approx. 3 – 5 hours' worth of time if you are researching everything as recommended.

It isn't always necessary to sell a poor performing property if research shows justifiable potential or opportunity for growth in the future. The blanket response of automatically selling can only be determined by doing the research and considering your options, so be wary of anyone suggesting this option without having provided individual analysis of the property. The costs of exiting and re-entering the property market are substantial, so make sure you do this as a best but last resort.

What to Do with a Dud Property

Like Justine above, once you have done your analysis, if it looks as though it's not going to improve and you choose to take no action, at least your expectations are now realistic as they are based on fact. You can now sleep at night (hopefully) because knowledge is power and you no longer have your head in the clouds.

Alternatively, if you wish to take some action, such as selling it, so you can free up your borrowing capacity, it is worth analysing what your break-even point will be once you take into account all of the 'exit' costs for selling the property (sales costs, capital gains tax if any, etc.), your entry costs for buying into your next property (stamp duty, legal etc.) and how long it will take based on an assumed capital growth rate and rental return (which ideally will perform above the average) to break even. It could be one year or five years, but at least by buying smarter next time and implementing the steps in this book, you will be well on your way to becoming a Prosperous Property Owner.

Reassess Your Beliefs around Money

Step 1 of this book was your Money Mindset, and I encourage you to review your beliefs around money regularly, especially if you aren't receiving the results you would like or need to achieve your lifestyle, personal or investment goals.

Simply go through the exercise in Step 1 on a regular basis (your yearly portfolio review could be a good opportunity) and notice whether the same beliefs come up, or whether there are new ones that need to be righted.

KEY POINTS

- Review your portfolio annually to ensure your property is still performing to expectation.

- Keep abreast of local events and economic issues that could be beneficial or detrimental to your portfolio's performance.

- Don't fall in love with your investment property, as this can lead you to make emotional decisions to your financial detriment.

- If your property is a 'lemon' then take appropriate action and seek expert advice. There's really no point sticking your head in the sand, as you are only guaranteeing your own failure. The right action will enable you to take back control of the situation and to take steps to turn it to your favour over time. Remember, inaction or indecision is actually a decision to do nothing.

NOTES

Conclusion

Next Steps

I believe there has never been a better time to provide investors with the information they need to create sustainable wealth via property investment, so that they can enjoy financial empowerment, achieve their financial goals and be in control of their future.

If you find yourself overwhelmed by what's required to create a sustainable property portfolio, don't let this stop you from investing. Simply make the decision to get professional help to enable you to progress. What this book will have highlighted is that it's not as easy to get it right as the magazines and property spruikers suggest. We all need professional help with different aspects of our lives and property is no different, so better to bite the bullet and get a positive result than do nothing and miss out on creating the financial security you desire.

There are plenty of investing opportunities in the marketplace and with some time and effort, it will be possible for you to create a sustainable property portfolio to achieve your financial goals. And, by reading this book, I trust that you are equipped to create a sustainable property investment strategy, and work with a team of experts who can fill your knowledge gaps. Working together, I know you can achieve property prosperity.

As outlined in this book, knowing who to trust and the right questions to ask can make all the difference to the outcome and success of your property investing journey. By asking these questions, you will be far more equipped to make informed investment decisions in future.

QUESTIONS TO ASK BEFORE ENGAGING A 'PROPERTY ADVISOR'

When researching property to buy, make sure you ask the following questions when attending any kind of meeting with a 'property advisor':

- What are you selling?

- Are you a Licensed Estate Agent or agent's representative?

- Is your company a licensed real estate agency, project marketer, investor or property 'club?'

- How do you/your company get paid and by whom? (They may say it's a 'marketing fee' or 'introduction fee' but they are really sales commissions.)

- Do you pay referral fees to third parties? (This applies if you have been referred by a third party such as a financial planner, accountant and mortgage broker or 'friend' who has recommended you investigate an opportunity). If so, how much will the third party earn if I buy the property?

- Do you charge me any fees? (Note – under each state's Estate Agents Act, a real estate agent can't legally take money from both parties to a transaction, even if they call it a 'buyer manger fee', 'membership fee' or similar, while also receiving a sales commission. If so, they should be reported to your local office of Fair Trading/ Consumer Affairs or the ACCC (Australian Competition and Consumer Commission) – see appendix 2.

- Are the membership fees actually a property reservation fee, what do my fees provide me with and under what circumstances are they refundable?

- Is the mentoring or coaching you provide unbiased and impartial? I.e. does the mentoring or coaching encourage me to buy only the property that you are selling or does it support me regardless of what and where I buy?

- As a 'research house', how and when do you make money?

- Why is this service for free and how do you make money?

- Are the property valuations you provide from independent firms or an in-house licensed property valuer? Who has paid for those 'independent' valuations and is there any reason why I can't get my own valuer to do one for me?

- If you charge me a fee and then rebate me the fee from the developer, who are you legally acting for in the property transaction?

And make sure you ask the 'property advisor' if they would still sell you this property if they got no money out of it. That way you will know if it's more about the money than the service or product they provide.

Trust your gut!

If for ANY reason you don't feel right about what is happening in the investment process or the speed at which it is happening, then step back and stop the process. Trust your gut feeling.

I use a lot of analysis when I work with clients to source and buy property for them as a Buyer Agent and APIA, however I also work intuitively and have come to trust that there is usually a legitimate reason if I don't like a property, even if I can't exactly put my finger on it at the time. It NEVER hurts to be cautious. If you are the sort of person who isn't assertive and feel you are being bullied into something, then please find someone who you trust who can be with you during the presentation process, and who can support you in asking for time or space to think about things. Remember, you can seek independent advice if you want or need it.

Also, do you TRUST the person you are dealing with and do you feel they genuinely have your best interests at heart? Being 'nice' isn't enough, you need to feel you trust them as you are spending hundreds of thousands. If the answer is no, then don't sign anything and take yourself out of the process. You can always step back in after you have had time to think, done your independent research or shown contracts to your solicitor/settlement agent/conveyancer and gotten their feedback, if you decide it is the best investment for you (meaning it meets all of you criteria, risk profile, circumstances, etc). Don't sign anything and rely on cooling off periods as this rushes you into making a decision you may not be ready for.

What if I bought a dud property?

If you purchased the property as a result of being referred by your advisor to a project wholesaler/marketer or property spruiker and it has proven to be a poor investment, remember you can always bring the matter to light with your advisor. You can also vote with your feet, change advisors, tell your friends about your experience and take your business elsewhere if they show no interest in your predicament. (Conversely, if the experience and the results have been exceptional and property performance has been above the average, then tell your friends about this positive scenario also!)

What Next?

If you are now fully informed, everything is transparent and you are comfortable with the supporting documentation you have been provided, then you simply need to make a decision as to whether you will proceed to purchase.

Remember that biased advice will never be the same as having independent and unbiased advice. However, if you follow the 7 Steps to Property Prosperity – fixing your money mindset, understanding your risk, developing a strategy, engaging your team of experts, doing your research, negotiating the offer, and regularly reviewing your portfolio – then you will have the knowledge and support to make informed investment decisions in future, and leverage your property to achieve your goals.

Now, GO FORTH AND PROSPER !

Appendix 1

Methods of Property Sales

As discussed in the introduction, referrers are professionals who refer their clients internally or externally to real estate marketers or promoters, and receive commissions each time one of their clients buys a property through the referred group. These professionals may include (but aren't limited to) accountants, financial planners, mortgage brokers and lawyers.

Typically the process works like this:

1 The wholesaler/aggregator/project marketer/spruiker aggressively markets to such professionals on the basis of setting up a property division in their practice, as a means of generating potentially hundreds of thousands or even millions of dollars in extra revenue for their business each year. Highly appealing for the professional, but at a risk to them! They provide motivational boot camps and systems to maximise client conversions – effectively turning your advisor into a property selling machine!

2 They provide 'referrer branded' websites and newsletters that promote the referrer's new property 'division' and streamline the sales process for them. They can provide 'In the Cloud' customer relationship managers and then operate the back-end of the business for them, providing innovative marketing tools and resources.

They could have a website portal set up where your accountant/broker/financial planner, etc. can directly access a variety of stock and price lists to select the property, print out investment reports, brochures, floor plans, etc. and get clients to 'reserve' property for a payment of a thousand dollars or more, with the view to buying in a few days' time.

3 Arrangements are then made to have contracts signed and often no special conditions are allowed to be inserted into the contract (because they don't work for you, they work for the vendor) and prices can't be negotiated for the same reason.

In some instances they may charge you a membership or upfront fee of thousands for a strategy or advice, but will rebate you the money once you purchase a property, so that it appears they are being paid by you and are impartial or unbiased. In fact they aren't, because this method still relies on you buying a property from them that they sell to you, for you to receive the rebate.

Or they could charge you a buyer manager, membership, mentoring or coaching fee which covers the cost of developing a property strategy and/or 'coordinating' all of the parties involved in the buying process including mortgage brokers, solicitors, property managers and quantity surveyors. Rest assured, there are many different fancy names that marketers use to distract you from the fact that you are probably paying a fee for something that could otherwise be free, or at least not have additional mark ups added to them.

Go to any property expo, summit or home show and you will see many examples of all of the above!

Telemarketing and E Marketing

Referrer clients could find themselves on the receiving end of phone calls or emails (sent via your advisor) inviting them to attend investment seminars or workshops, either online or in person.

1   At these presentations you are shown 'property based' strategies (often only relating to the property they have to sell) on how you can create wealth (not unlike those meeting with coaches, mentors, research houses), your borrowing capacity is assessed and you are presented with 'exclusive' properties to buy. This either happens directly with your advisor (they get a bigger commission if they are involved) or you are introduced to a third party who takes you through the property selection process.

2   They often provide lending and legal solutions via a one-stop-shop, which in theory means they are meant to

advise you as you are paying them to do so, so ask the conveyancer which clauses to REMOVE from the contract to provide you with more protection. It's possible that they may not provide advice regarding the property if you don't ask specific questions, especially if the developer or project market provides the majority of their clientele, so independent experts are always a better option, even if you have to pay.

Real Estate Regulations and Professional Indemnity Insurance

What most investors don't realise is that real estate professional indemnity insurance is cover for the real estate transaction, i.e. the transfer of the title between parties, and it makes NO provision for the supply of 'property advice'. A referrer sharing commissions is technically acting under real estate law, because the party they take their fees from determines which party they are acting for, therefore anyone taking fees is vulnerable to being sued by their clients. Also their professional indemnity insurance won't likely cover them if they are performing outside of their professional capacity.

When referrers take kickbacks or fees from a builder for the 'improvement' of the land (i.e. the building) instead of the real estate transaction (i.e. house and land complete packages), they don't have to meet the real estate regulations and disclose the commissions being paid to the referrer, so again there is a lack of transparency.

As always, Buyer Beware

Appendix 2

USEFUL RESOURCES

Miriam's Buyer Advocacy and Property Investment Advice
Property Mavens
(03) 9988 2266
www.propertymavens.com.au

Register on the website to access a supply of continually updated free resources and to keep up to date with Miriam's regular property blog.

Education for Professionals
Accountants, financial planners and mortgage brokers can take Miriam's short 'Property Advice Course' to ensure you are having better informed property investing conversations with your clients.
The course is in collaboration with Registered Training Organisation – Mentor Education.

Mentor Education
Property Advice Course
1300 054 253
www.mentor.edu.au

ABS Population

http://www.abs.gov.au/ausstats/abs@.nsf/Products/3218.0
~2010-11~Main+Features~Victoria?OpenDocument

Go to download tab to view range or reports available.

ABS Housing Starts

http://www.abs.gov.au/ausstats/abs@.nsf/mf/8731.0

Go to downloads tab to view range of reports available.

ABS Average Weekly Earnings

http://www.abs.gov.au/ausstats/abs@.nsf/mf/6302.0/

Professional Property Data

Core Logic RP Data
www.corelogic.com.au

Australian Property Monitors

http://apm.com.au/

Hotspotting Research Reports

www.hotspotting.com.au

Residex

http://www.residex.com.au/

Valuer General's Department, reports

http://www.dse.vic.gov.au/property-titles-and-maps/
valuation-home-page

RPD Nationwide

http://www.prdnationwide.com.au/research/report_search/
region/Australia/sort/dated/size/10/default.aspx

Local research

Port Authority

Airport Authority

Local Councils

Chamber of Commerce

Major businesses such as resource companies

State Government authorities such as Roads, Planning,
Infrastructure.

Other

Archicentre

www.archicentre.com.au

Archicentre offers architectural services to home buyers,
new home builders and renovators.

Australian Bureau of Statistics

www.abs.gov.au

The Australian Bureau of Statistics (ABS) website provides
a wide variety of Australian statistics including information
about housing and demographics.

Australian Institute of Quantity Surveyors (A1QS)

www.aiqs.com.au

The AIQS is a professional body that aims to maintain standards of professionalism among quantity surveyors. It can also help you find a surveyor.

Australian Property Institute (API)

www.api.org.au

The API sets and maintains standards of professional practice, education, ethics and professional conduct for its members and the property profession more generally.

Australian Property Monitors (APM)

www.apm.com.au

Australian Property Monitors provides online property price information. Its website features various price guide reports from across the country.

Australian Taxation Office (ATO)

www.ato.gov.au

The ATO website has tax-related information for property investors, from declarable income to claimable items at tax time.

Domain.com.au

www.domain.com.au

Domain.com.au provides tools and information for buyers, sellers and renters Australia-wide.

Property.com.au

www.property.com.au

Property.com.au is a search engine for real estate that provides the option to view properties on realestate.com.au and (in almost all cases) directly on the real estate agent's website.

Property Council of Australia (PCA)

www.propertyoz.com.au

PCA represents the property community, those who use land or invest in the built environment to generate economic returns.

Realestate.com.au

www.realestate.com.au

Realestate.com.au is a property-based website, listing real estate for sale, and other property listings by real estate agents.

Realestateview

realestateview.com.au

Realestateview is a joint venture between Real Estate Institutes of Australia and real estate agents. It advertises homes for sale, rental properties and holiday rentals.

Residex

www.residex.com.au

Residex provides Australian residential property statistics based on sales back to 1901 and offers predictions for future property growth. There is a cost to access most reports.

Core Logic RP Data
www.corelogic.com.au
RP Data is a members only website that offers comprehensive Australia-wide property information.

Real Estate Institute of Australia
STATE BRANCHES

1 Real Estate Institute of the ACT
www.reiact.com.au
Street address: Ground Floor, 16, Thesiger Court, Deakin West, ACT 2600
Phone: (02) 6282 4544 Fax: (02) 6285 1960
Email: info@reiact.com.au

2 Real Estate Institute of Victoria
www.reiv.com.au
Phone: (03) 9205 6666 Fax: (03) 9205 6699
Street address: 335 Camberwell Rd, Camberwell, Vic. 3124
Email: reiv@reiv.com.au

3 Real Estate Institute of NSW
www.reinsw.com.au

30-32 Wentworth Ave, Sydney South, NSW 2000
Phone: (02) 9264 2343 Fax: (02) 9267 9190
Email: info@reinsw.com.au

4 **Real Estate Institute of Northern Territory**
www.reint.com.au
Street address: Real Estate House Unit 3, 6 Lindsay Street Darwin, NT 0800
Phone: (08) 8981 8905

5 **Real Estate Institute of Queensland**
www.reiq.com.au
Street Address; 21 Turbo Drive, Coorparoo, Qld 4151
Phone: (07) 3249 7347 Fax: (07) 3249 6211

6 **Real Estate Institute of Western Australia**
www.reiwa.com
Street address: REIWA House, 215 Hay Street, Subiaco, WA 6008
Phone: (08) 9380 8222 Fax: (08) 9381 9260
Email: reiwa.com@reiwa.com.au

7 **Real Estate Institute of South Australia**
www.reisa.com.au
Street Address; REI House, 249 Greenhill Road, Dulwich, SA 5065
Phone: (08) 8366 4300 Fax (08) 8366 4380
Email: reisa@reisa.com.au

8 Real Estate Institute of Tasmania

www.reit.com.au

Address: 33 Melville St, Hobart, Tas. 7000

Phone: (03) 6223 4769 Fax: (03) 6223 7748

Email: admin@relt.com.au

Property Investment Association of Australia (PIAA)

PIAA was formed in response to serious concerns about the lack of transparency and professionalism in the property investment advice sector. Investors were being exposed to real estate selling tactics and being channelled into unsustainable property holdings that didn't support their life time wealth creation. Many were effectively being fleeced of their accumulated capital.

PIAA began as an investors' association focused on the new standards identified by the Joint Houses Parliamentary Enquiry post Henry Kaye, Safe as Houses. It has since morphed into a professional association with a strong focus on professional standards including the FOFA* legislation.

It has pioneered a range of initiatives including:

1 Property Information Standardisation

This supports investor comparison of property investment opportunities based on their factual merits rather than their emotional appeal.

This took the form of a Due Diligence Audit to rate off the plan investments. It covered over 200 categories of information and the results were reported as a five star rating. This required independence and kept the profile of this organisation low. This process is now managed by an external company.

2 Professional Support for Advisors

ASIC is the current regulator of professional advice for other asset classes and borrowing. Their professional standards for these groups are:

- an educational qualification,
- professional indemnity insurance, and,
- membership of a professional association.

PIAA has adopted these standards.

3 Education

PIAA developed a professional property investment advice course based around a business process that delivers transparent and professional advice to clients to help them make better investment decisions. The course is in its fifth year and has had great testimonials from participants from mortgage broking, accounting, financial planning, legal and property investment advice sectors.

4 Professional Indemnity Insurance

PIAA graduates can apply for a bespoke PI insurance policy for their advice component. This is vital to support recourse in the unlikely event of a client complaint. It also supports referring solicitors, financial planners, mortgage professionals and accountants cover the gap that has traditionally been unmanaged via referrals to selling agents.

5 Professional Associations

PIAA became a professional association in June 2012. It provides regulatory, PI insurance and educational support for its members. Visit our website at www.piaa.asn.au or call (02) 9499 9499 to ask for your nearest advisor.
*FOFA: the Future of Financial Advice.

The Real Estate Buyer's Agents Association of Australia (REBAA) was established in 2000 with the goal to raise the profile of the industry and to establish guidelines for the professional conduct of real estate buyer's agents nationally.

Buyer's agents are licensed professionals who specialise in searching, negotiating and purchasing property on behalf of buyers

As a leading player in the property industry, REBAA offers significant benefits to both buyer's agents and consumers.

REBAA operates as a national network with accredited members all over Australia.

By choosing a REBAA accredited member, buyers can be confident they are dealing with a professional and fully licensed buyer's agent.

Visit the website to find your nearest accredited REBAA member www.rebaa.com.au

Appendix 3

Common Property Investment and Development Risks

Please remember that the risks associated with property investment can be extensive, and I'm only touching the surface with some of the risks identified below. Please ensure you undertake thorough research before you proceed with any investment.

Market Value Risk

Market value risk is the risk of an investment failing to achieve its expected growth. Much of the information that marketers use to make a sale predicts a certain rate of return, however, these returns can be impacted by both known and unknown risks.

This could result in the re-sale value of an investment not achieving the expected return, particularly if the owner chooses to sell before, during or following depressed market activity, when properties settle and valuations don't often stack up to the purchase price. This results in investors having to put in more equity to make up the shortfall OR they simply can't settle (see settlement risk).

Market value risk can apply to the following property investment strategies – off the plan properties, land banking, renovating to add value, house and land packages and the National Rental Affordability Scheme (NRAS). To learn more about these property types and strategies, refer to Step 5 Research, Select and Assess.

Construction Risk

Construction risk applies to properties purchased off the plan, house and land packages and the NRAS (refer Step 5 Research, Select and Assess). Throughout such projects the developer may arrange finance facilities related to the land acquisition, development and construction of the project. This may result in issues arising in the timely delivery of the project and as specified in the contracted terms. Delays in the delivery period could result in opportunity costs as investors' funds may not be able to be redirected to alternative investments.

Settlement Risk

Settlement risks may prevent the purchaser's ability to settle on the property. Typically, these are related to difficulties in obtaining finance either through valuation shortfalls at the time of settlement, or changes in the purchaser's personal circumstances. This may result in the loss of the deposit or any monies owed to the developer, and could even result in the loss of a sale altogether, forcing an investor to resell a property in a depressed market for a lower amount. A settlement that falls through could also require legal action to be taken against the defaulting purchaser.

This risk may be managed by obtaining pre-approval of finance (for completed property) prior to the exchange of contracts; however, this is never a guarantee of obtaining the finance at settlement as personal circumstances could still change.

Settlement risk can apply to the following property investment strategies – off the plan properties, developing, renovating to add value, house and land packages and NRAS. For more information on each of these, refer to Step 5 Research, Select and Assess.

Developer Risk
Inexperienced developers can spell disaster for investors, so ensure you do your due diligence when investing in off the plan properties, developing, house and land packages and NRAS (learn more about these investment strategies at Step 5 Research, Select and Assess).

Who is the developer and what is their track record? How many of this type of property have they built before and what is their reputation in the marketplace? Who is the architect designing the project, have they designed this type of project before, and how is their track record and reputation? And finally, what are the sunset clauses in the contract that allow the developer to walk away without penalty, when you, as the buyer, have committed to the purchase, resulting in a potentially huge opportunity cost?

Builder Risk

As per developer risk, a project's builder can have a significant impact on the return of your investment, particularly when investing in off the plan properties, developing, house and land packages and NRAS.

Remember to ask who the builder is, and how their track record is. How many of this type of property have they built, and do they have a good reputation in the marketplace? Are there completed examples of their work where you can check the quality of the build? Are there testimonials you can obtain from previous clients? What are their financials like in terms of liquidity and their ability to manage funds that you pay them incrementally throughout the construction process?

Additional Risk Considerations

Rental Yield Risk

Rental yields fluctuate due to factors such as supply, demand, employment, investment in the area and the state of the overall residential market. This is particularly relevant if you are investing in property to generate passive income through rental yields.

Personal Risk

Investment strategies often depend on the income of the investor. Should there be a reduction or loss in an investor's income, it may present a risk in the future ability to hold the investment. These risks may be managed through the appropriate use of income protection insurance, life insurance and trauma insurance.

Interest Rate Risk

Movements in interest rates can have a number of effects on an individual property investment. Specifically, a rate increase may immediately increase the costs of holding an investment property. Additionally, sustained interest rate rises may have a lagging effect in the form of reduced sales activity and property growth. Seek advice from your finance broker about the pros and cons of fixing your interest rates.

Policy Risk

Changes in government policy and infrastructure spending may affect both holding costs and the expected growth performance of specific property investments. This may result in additional expenditure in order to finance your portfolio and the expected returns.

Oversupply

An oversupply in property will have effects on both achievable rents and growth performance. Due to the length of time typically required to construct medium and high density developments, the short-term supply curve is inelastic. This means that property supply has an inherent inability to adjust quickly enough to meet demand. A sudden reduction in demand or an unexpected increase in supply may result in oversupply. Typically this risk is most acute towards the end of the property cycle.

Lending

Loans will need to be obtained for each property purchase and there may be a point in time where your borrowing capacity is maxed out. This may require a commercial lending approach. A specialist mortgage broker would need to be consulted progressively throughout the implementation of the investment strategy.

Development Risk Considerations

Acquisition Risk

Acquisition risk is the cost of acquiring a development site and a viable Development Approval (DA). As the DA will determine the number of dwellings that can be built on the site, the true viability and feasibility of the project can't be determined until the DA has been approved and issued. To minimise the risk of lack of viability, developers will often secure a development site using an option contract and may make one of the conditions of the purchase as being subject to obtaining a DA.

Marketing Risk

When investing in property developments, marketing risk is the developer's ability to market and sell properties before construction, as this provides greater security in relation to completing the project.

If sales aren't made, entire projects can languish. Building contracts can expire or need to be requoted. Increases in building costs can then render a development no longer viable, so sales are imperative as money isn't made by the developer until the project is completed and the contracts are settled.

Finance Risk

A developer may not qualify for finance or may not be able to arrange finance facilities related to the land acquisition, development and construction of the project. This may result in issues arising in the delivery of the product on time and as specified in the contracted terms. Delays in the delivery period could result in additional costs. They may also require that the developer hold or land bank the property until the opportunity for finance arises and, if that is unlikely, the developer might need to sell the property. Lenders often also require a minimum percentage of sales to have been made before finance is approved. Often the riskier the development (e.g. a high rise apartment tower) the higher the required level of pre-sales (e.g. 70% to obtain funding).

Developer Risk

Inexperienced developers can spell disaster for investors, so ensure you do your due diligence. Who is the developer and what is their track record? How many of this type of property have they built before and what is their reputation in the publicly? Who is the architect designing the project, have they designed this type of project before, and how is their track record and reputation? And finally, what are the sunset clauses in the contract that allow the developer to walk away without penalty, when you, as the buyer, have committed to the purchase, resulting in a potentially huge opportunity cost?

Builder Risk

As per the developer risk, who is the builder and what is their track record? How many of this type of property/ development have they built before and what is their reputation in the publicly like re delivering on time and to budget? Are there completed examples of their work that you can look at to check the quality of the build and testimonials you can obtain from previous clients? What are their financials like in terms of liquidity and their ability to manage funds that you pay them incrementally throughout the construction process?

Settlement Risk

Settlement risk includes the purchaser's ability to settle on the property. Typically, these are related to difficulties in obtaining finance either through valuation shortfalls at the time of settlement or changes in the purchaser's personal circumstances that result in the refusal of the purchaser's credit application. This may result in the loss of the sale and the need to resell the property in a depressed market for a lower amount, therefore potentially requiring legal action to be taken against the defaulting purchaser.

General Risk
In addition to the risk factors specific to investing in property developments, there are more general risks that can affect the value of an investment in the development, including:

- The state of Australia's and the world economies
- Movements in inflation and employment
- Changes in socio-economic factors
- Natural or man-made disasters (e.g. recent national flooding)

To learn more about developing as an investment strategy, refer to Developing at Step 5 Research, Select and Assess.

Appendix 4

INVESTMENT ATTITUDES

How concerned are you about the security of your capital?

Extremely	1	2	3	4	5	6	7	8	9	10	Not

How important is it that the growth of your investments beats inflation?

Extremely	1	2	3	4	5	6	7	8	9	10	Not

How concerned are you about the impact of taxation on your investment returns?

Extremely	1	2	3	4	5	6	7	8	9	10	Not

How important is it to maximise the potential of your investment performance?

Extremely	1	2	3	4	5	6	7	8	9	10	Not

How concerned are you about rises and falls in the capital value of your investments?

Extremely	1	2	3	4	5	6	7	8	9	10	Not

How important is it for you to be able to cash in your investments at any time?

Extremely	1	2	3	4	5	6	7	8	9	10	Not

What level of involvement do you require?

Passive	Medium	Active

INVESTOR TYPE - WHAT TYPE OF INVESTOR ARE YOU?

Conservative

Investors seeking a relatively low risk investment over a moderate time frame. They are prepared to accept lower returns to preserve capital. The adverse effects of tax and inflation are not a concern, provided the initial investment is protected.

☐

Cautious

Investors seeking better than basic returns, with low risk over a moderate time frame. They are willing to accept modest exposure to less aggressive growth investments to achieve a higher return than the conservative portfolio and cash.

☐

Prudent

Investors wanting a balanced portfolio of diversified investments to meet medium to long term financial goals. They require a strategy, which will cope with the effects of tax inflation Calculated risks are acceptable to achieve greater returns.

☐

Assertive

Investors wanting to invest funds for capital growth over the medium to long term through a diversified portfolio. They are willing to accept more aggressive/growth investments with higher volatility (and the potential for capital loss in the short term).

☐

Aggressive

Investors prepared to compromise portfolio balance to pursue potentially higher long-term gains. Your investment choices are diverse but carry with them a higher level of risk. Security of capital is secondary to the potential wealth accumulation.

☐

RISK ATTITUDES

Please indicate how you would rate the importance of protecting against the following:

Low Priority

High Priority

	1	2	3	4	5	6	7	8	9	10
Loss/damage to house	1	2	3	4	5	6	7	8	9	10
Loss/damage to vehicles	1	2	3	4	5	6	7	8	9	10
Loss/damage to personal/property	1	2	3	4	5	6	7	8	9	10
Severe illness/loss of health	1	2	3	4	5	6	7	8	9	10
Loss of income	1	2	3	4	5	6	7	8	9	10
Loss of life	1	2	3	4	5	6	7	8	9	10
Total and permanent disability	1	2	3	4	5	6	7	8	9	10
Loss of business interests	1	2	3	4	5	6	7	8	9	10

GLOSSARY OF TERMS

Auction - a method of selling real estate, via a public bidding process.

Australian Securities and Investments Commission (ASIC) - ASIC is an independent Commonwealth government body that regulates Australia's corporations, markets and the financial services sector, including financial planning, insurance and mortgage broking.

Borrower - a party to a loan - the person or entity borrowing the funds.

Buyer's agent /advocate - a licensed real estate professional who legally acts for a buyer to research, source and/or negotiate for property on a fee for service basis.

Buying off the plan – is when you purchase a property based on a set of plans and a design concept, before it has been constructed, or at varying stages of construction.

Capital Gains Tax (CGT) - CGT is a cost of investing. You pay CGT on the gain made upon the sale of an income-producing asset. The methods for calculating CGT may differ from time to time and depend upon when the asset was acquired and in what type of entity it was purchased e.g. individual name versus company versus SMSF.

Cash flow - the amount of money remaining, or owing, after rent is collected, expenses are paid and tax claims are made. The amount will be either positive (if money is left over) or negative (if money is owed).

Central Business District (CBD) - this is the main commercial area of a city or large regional town.

Contract of sale - a legal document that outlines the terms and conditions relating to the sale of a property.

Cooling-off period – a short, specified period of time when the buyer can unconditionally withdraw from an executed contract of sale.

Depreciation - refers to the loss in value of an asset, due to general wear and tear and the effects of time on the building, fixtures, fittings and furniture on an eligible, income-producing property. The age of a property will affect both whether such claims are available to you, what claims can be made and how much they are.

Developer - an individual or company that takes the risk of improving the value of land by building on it, with the express purpose of making a profit.

Equity - the difference between what you owe and what you own of a property.

Exit strategy – a plan of action developed by an investor before purchasing property, with the intent to sell their property at a later date and in conjunction with their overall strategy.

Fixtures and fittings – fixtures are physically secured Items that are usually included with the sale of a property, such as carpets, built in wardrobes, gas and electrical fittings and curtains. Fittings are not normally included in a contract if they can be removed without causing damage, so they need to be specified as being part of the chattels for sale in the contract of sale.

Freehold title - an example of clear title. This means that once you buy the property, no-one can come along and claim that the title is not yours (also see Torrens Title, Green Title).

Gearing - 'to borrow' funds for the purpose of investing in property or other assets. It is often deemed 'negative' or 'positive' (please see negative gearing and positive gearing).

Growth drivers - the factors which affect asset growth. They are economic influences which are created by a set of circumstances, rather than single, individual events, which can be repeated and sustained over time and which are a sign of underlying economic growth.

Housing starts - the number of new private dwellings where construction has commenced in a given period of time - most often measured quarterly.

Income - revenue or money earned through investment return or work.

Interest - a sum charged by the lender, calculated at a % rate on the outstanding balance of borrowings, in exchange for having supplied you with funds.

Joint and several liability – when you buy a property in partnership and borrow funds to do so, you each own a portion of the property but are each 100% liable for the debt.

Landlord - the owner of a rental property, be it residential, commercial or industrial.

Landlord's insurance - insurance taken out by a property owner to protect against tenant damage or income/rent default.

Lease agreement - a legally binding written agreement between a tenant and landlord that outlines the terms of the lease, including providing possession of a property for a given period without conferring ownership.

Lender - a business or collective group that lends funds to enable a borrower to buy a property.

Leveraging - the use of borrowed funds for the purpose of investing

Loan to Valuation Ratio (LVR) - this is ratio which measures the percentage that a lender will lend to a borrower in relation to what percentage of the loan the borrower will fund. For example, if the LVR on an investment property is 80% and the property is valued at $400,000, the lender will advance $320,000 and the borrower must fund the different of 20% or $80,000 of the investment.

Market value - the value of a property based on what a competitive marketplace is willing to pay.

Macro economy - this is the economic 'big picture' based on national or state economic data.

Median price - is the measurement of property prices within a certain geographical area or property class, based on the middle price point and determined when prices are arranged from highest to lowest during a particular timeframe e.g. monthly or quarterly.

Micro economy - this is the economic small picture of an area where you are researching to buy and includes population growth; business; demographics; infrastructure plans of the area.

Mortgage - a legally binding agreement whereby the lender takes security over the property in exchange for providing funds in the form of a loan. The document identifies the terms and conditions of a loan.

Mortgage broker - an independent professional who assists borrowers to choose and secure a home loan from an independent lender.

Negative gearing - when income from a rental property is less than the costs associated with owning and maintaining that property (including mortgage payments). It is not a 'strategy', but a tax term.

Owner occupied - where the owner of a property also resides in it.

Passed in - when a property is not sold at public auction because the bidding did not reach the seller's minimum reserve price.

Positive cash flow is when you are left with money after you claim all of your tax deductions. This can happen when you negatively gear (and subsequently get a tax break larger than the loss) or where you positively gear (where you have money left over after you have paid the tax on any rental income you have made).

Positive gearing - when income from a rental property is greater than the costs associated with owning and maintaining that property. It is not a 'strategy', it is a tax term.

Private sale/treaty - when a property is sold through private sale method, usually via a real estate agent.

Property manager - a person who manages a rental property - they can be the owner or a professional and licensed real estate agent who is paid a fee for the service.

Quantity surveyor - a person who consults on construction costs and depreciation schedules for property owners.

Reserve price - the lowest price at which a seller is willing to sell a property.

Rent guarantee - a promise to pay a pre-agreed rent for a pre-agreed term.

Risk tolerance - the level of risk with which investors are willing to incur loss in exchange for return via investing. It is determined based on their responses to a series of questions about how they feel about investing and their personal investing choices.

Settlement - the date when the balance of a contract price is paid to the vendor and the buyer legally a buyer takes ownership of a property due to a transfer of title.

Self-Managed Superannuation Funds (SMSFs) - a self-managed super fund (SMSF) is a trust established for one to four people where cash and investments are held for the principal purpose of funding the members' retirement. The costs of setting up a fund can be prohibitive and the compliance onerous.

Strata title - a title usually applied to property within a multi-unit property scheme, such as a group of flats or apartments. By law, an owners' corporation, or body corporate, must be formed and every single owner given the right to membership of that entity.

Stamp duty - a state-based tax charged on property (and other commercial) transactions.

Stratum title - a title that can be applied to units and apartments owned by a company. Owners receive a registered title to their property within the development.

Subdivision - the legal act of dividing land into individual components recognised under separate titles, which can be sold off individually.

Tenant - either the person signing a lease to occupy premises to live in, in exchange for paying rent or the description of a party to a property title.

Title (of property) - the legal document recording a person's right to ownership of a property. There are various forms of title, with particular characteristics (also see Freehold, Torrens Title, Green Title, Strata, Company, Community and Old System Title).

Vacancy rate - the percentage of the year during which a property remains vacant. This is usually ascertained by dividing the number of weeks the property is vacant by the number of weeks in the year (52) or the percentage of available rental properties that are vacant at a given point in time

Valuation - a professional assessment of a property's value at a given point in time which is documented in the form of a sworn valuation.

Vendor - the person(s) or entity selling a property.

Index

Accountant 90, 104-108, 112,
145
Concerning SMSFs 157,
159
'Free' property advice 4, 7
Referrers 14-16, 205, 211-
214
Accredited Property
Investment Advisor 51, 71,
91-95, 98, 104
Property investing models
5-7
Auctions 180-188, 242

Buyer agent representative
100
Buying unconditionally 145-
146
Passing in 182-184
Price negotiations 180-181
Reserve price 169-170
Underquoting 171-174
Building inspector 117-120

Buyer advocate 23, 48, 95,
96, 98

Buyer agent 91, 95-104, 118-
120, 159, 207
Property investing models
5-7

Conveyancer 106, 112-113,
208, 214

Economy
Macroeconomics 95, 160,
162, 246
Microeconomics 94, 160, 161,
162, 197, 246

Financial planner 107, 108-
109, 157, 159
Concerning SMSFs 157,
159
'Free' property advice 4, 7
Mitigating risk 41, 110
Referrers 14-16, 112, 205,
211-214

Gearing 244
Positive 248
Negative 21, 44, 45, 57,
58, 59, 60, 78, 77-79,
83, 107, 163, 244

Insurance 8, 47, 58, 70, 80, 108, 126, 233, 242
    Broker 124-126
    Landlord's 126, 245
    Professional indemnity 3, 92, 93, 97, 99, 122, 214-215, 225
    Underinsurance 125, 126
Interest (rates) 58, 73, 74, 77, 79, 82, 93, 109, 111, 158, 233, 245
Investor types 41-45
Investor attitudes 41-45
    Personal risk 40, 41, 41-45, 61, 132, 140, 233
    Risk appetite 48-52, 61, 94
    Risk attitude 46-48, 61

Markets 10, 16, 21, 80-82, 147
    Australian property market 24
    Conditions 54, 75, 81, 160
    Cycles 80-82
    Oversupply 21, 155, 161, 193, 194, 233, 234
    Timing 80-82

Mortgage broker 4, 7, 14, 26, 51, 93, 109-112, 205, 211, 212, 234, 247
Money mindset 30-37, 132, 199, 209

Negotiating 52, 96, 100, 174, 175-187, 209

Pest inspector 93, 104, 120
Property advertising 19, 169-170, 180
Property manager 22, 72, 93, 99, 101, 121-123, 150, 156, 213, 248
Property sale methods
    Coaching/Mentoring 10, 12, 18, 206, 213
    Enticements 21-22
    Referrers 10, 14-15, 112, 136, 211-215
    Research houses 10, 15-16, 163, 206, 213
    Telemarketing 10, 17, 213
Property investment types 132-160

Developing 40, 53, 61, 141-146, 209, 231, 232, 236-237

Established property 20, 97, 132, 133-136, 153

House and land packages 152-153

Land banking 9, 12, 146-147, 230, 235

Lease options 55, 150-152

National Rental Affordability Scheme (NRAS) 53, 78, 92, 153-157, 159, 163, 230, 231, 232

Off the plan 6, 55, 56, 79, 97, 132, 136, 137-141, 142, 153, 154, 159, 225, 230, 231, 225, 242

Renovating 55, 145, 148, 151, 230, 231

Self-Managed Superfunds (SMSFs) 16, 22, 108, 157-160, 163, 249

Quantity surveyor 90, 127, 128, 213, 220, 248

Real estate agent 4, 7, 8, 13, 97, 177, 206

Regulation 71, 106, 156, 214, 215

Consumer Affairs 8, 11, 17, 96, 168, 172, 206

Real Estate Act 96, 206

Real Estate Institute 96, 97, 121-122, 168, 222-224

Real Estate Institute of Victoria (REIV) 168, 222

Real estate law 99, 125, 177, 214

Rental income statistics 77-78

Retirement income 66-75, 82, 157

Retire on rents 71-72

Refinance into retirement 67, 72-74

Selling 74-75

Risk

Appetite 48-52, 61, 94

Attitude 46-48, 61

Mitigation

Types of 133-160, 229-237

Acquisition risk 234

Builder risk 232, 236

Construction risk 230

Developer risk 231-232, 236

Finance risk 235

General risk 237

Interest rate risk 233

Lending 223

Market value risk 229-230

Marketing risk 235

Oversupply 233-234

Personal risk 233

Policy risk 233

Rental yield risk 232

Settlement risk 230-231, 236-237

Settlement agent 112-115, 208

Solicitor 20, 21, 93, 95, 104, 106, 112-115, 208, 213, 226

Strategies 5-7, 12-13, 16, 17, 40, 46, 47, 52, 53-61, 66-75, 80, 83, 88, 91, 92, 93, 106, 132-160, 163, 180, 195, 212, 213, 229, 230, 231, 233

10 in 10 149-150

Capital growth 57-59

Cash-flow 59-60

Combined 60

Entry strategies 69

Hold strategies 69-70

Long-term strategies 54, 94

Property usage 54

Retire on rents 71-72

Refinance into retirement 67, 72-74

Selling 74-75

Short-term strategies 54-56, 80, 150

Underquoting 169, 170-173

ABOUT THE AUTHOR

CEO & Founder Property Mavens
Licensed Buyers' Agent / Licensed
Estate Agent (Vic)
Accredited Property Investment
Advisor (APIA)
Best selling author
Multi industry trainer and educator
Diploma of Property
Diploma of Business Studies
Media Commentator

With a background in the financial services industry, it was purchasing her first property at age 23 which set Miriam Sandkuhler on the path to property prosperity.

But it wasn't all smooth sailing. By making some costly but enlightening mistakes, which taught her more than any seminar, Miriam has built a unique breadth of knowledge which she now shares with corporate and individual investors via her firm: www.propertymavens.com.au.

Miriam has turned a weakness into her key strength: by learning the hard way what an 'investment grade' property is, she can teach you to see through the common pitfalls that hoodwink even the best of us.

Miriam's trademark is independent, unbiased advice minus the marketing spin. She takes personal pride in supporting clients to make sustainable, strategic decisions on investment properties with the least amount of risk and stress.

An Accredited Property Investment Advisor, Licensed Estate Agent, REIV member and award nominated Buyer Agent, REBAA and PIAA member, Miriam walks her talk. With nearly twenty years of professional real estate experience in two different states, and having sold and bought many millions of dollars' worth of property for clients, Miriam is well-versed at what makes a high-performing investment-grade property, and how to strategically build a sustainable and prosperous property portfolio.

She is passionate about educating consumers and professional financial advisors (via her Property Advice Course and workshops). Working directly with property investors and professional financial advisor clients, Miriam helps them to become empowered, financially secure and in control of their future.

Miriam's Amazon #1 best selling book, Property Prosperity, is essential reading for anyone wanting clear, accessible advice on property investment in Australia. Packed with case studies, exercises and real-life experience and examples, Property Prosperity truly means everyone can benefit from Miriam's extensive experience.

When she's not working with clients on their next property purchase, Miriam makes the most of Melbourne's bounty of cultural and creative options for socialising and keeping fit.

Miriam is also 'aunty' to a poodle cross pooch called Molly, who she shares with her neighbour, a win-win situation for all!

www.ingramcontent.com/pod-product-compliance
Lightning Source LLC
Chambersburg PA
CBHW060237220326
41598CB00027B/3969